Presented
with the compliments of
Glaxo Laboratories Limited

To _____

By _____ *Bill Matthews* _____

Glaxo ✠

DISEASES OF THE OESOPHAGUS, STOMACH AND DUODENUM

A guide to diagnosis

DISEASES OF THE OESOPHAGUS, STOMACH AND DUODENUM

A guide to diagnosis

J.J. Misiewicz C.I. Bartram P.B. Cotton
A.S. Mee A.B. Price R.P.H. Thompson

 **Glaxo** Glaxo Laboratories Limited

Produced and published by
Gower Medical Publishing London UK for
Glaxo Laboratories Limited Greenford Middlesex UK

Project Editor: David Bennet

Art Director: G. Max Dyson

Illustration: Pamela Corfield

ISBN 0-906923-28-X

© Copyright 1986 by Gower Medical Publishing Limited.
Middlesex House, 34-42 Cleveland Street, London W1P 5FB, UK.

The sponsorship of this book does not imply approval or otherwise of any
of the products of the sponsor by the authors or contributors.

Printed in Italy by Imago Publishing Ltd.

Preface

The text and illustrations contained in this handbook provide extensive visual documentation of the normal anatomy, histology, endoscopy and radiology. The text and illustrations were not intended as a textbook of gastrointestinal disease and should not be used, or judged, as such. Instead, the notes and illustrations form a convenient aide memoire to remind the reader of various aspects of normal and abnormal gastrointestinal function and anatomy.

Gastroenterology is progressing and developing rapidly, and technological advances in imaging techniques of the alimentary tract have played an important part in the advance of the subject. Diagnostic procedures and methods are described, and histopathological treated in some detail, reflecting the importance of histopathological evaluation in alimentary disease, for example in the area of pre-cancerous conditions.

It has been a great pleasure to join with my fellow editors in the production of this handbook which I hope will prove useful to many of our colleagues.

J.J. Misiewicz
Department of Gastroenterology and Nutrition
Central Middlesex Hospital
London, England

Authors

J.J. Misiewicz
BSc, MB, FRCP
Consultant Physician and
Head of Department of Gastroenterology and Nutrition,
Central Middlesex Hospital, London, U.K.

C.I. Bartram
MB BS, MRCP, FRCR
Consultant Radiologist,
St. Mark's and St. Bartholomew's Hospitals, London, U.K.

P.B. Cotton
MD, FRCP
Consultant Physician,
The Middlesex Hospital, London, U.K.

A.S. Mee
MD, MRCP
Consultant Physician,
The Battle Hospital, Reading, U.K.

A.B. Price
MA, BM, BCh, MRCPath
Consultant Pathologist,
Northwick Park Hospital and C.R.C., Harrow, U.K.

R.P.H. Thompson
DM, FRCP
Consultant Physician,
St. Thomas' Hospital, London, U.K.

Contents

1. The Normal Oesophagus and Stomach

2. Oesophageal Disease

3. Diseases of the Stomach

4. Normal Duodenum and Duodenal Disease

1.
The Normal Oesophagus and Stomach

Normal Oesophagus

The oesophagus is a muscular tube connecting the oropharynx to the stomach. It begins at the lower margin of the cricopharyngeus muscle and is approximimately 25cm in length. It is composed of striated muscle in its upper third, smooth muscle in the lower two thirds and is lined by squamous epithelium.

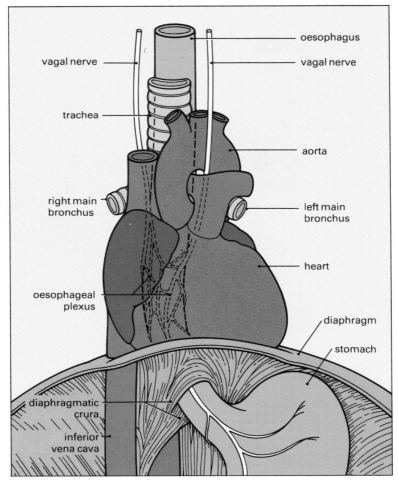

Fig.1.1 Diagram showing the anatomical relations of the oesophagus.

In the mediastinum the oesophagus is closely related to the two trunks of the vagus nerve, the trachea, aorta and the heart (Figs. 1.1 & 1.2) so that both bronchial and aortic impressions can be seen during a barium

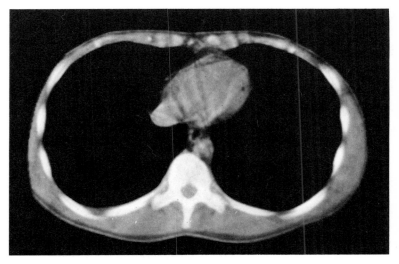

Fig.1.2 Transverse computerised tomographic (CT) scan of the thorax at the level of T4.

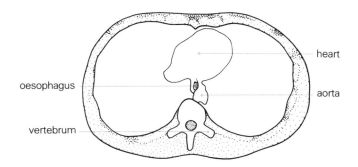

oesophagus

heart

aorta

vertebrum

swallow examination (Fig.1.3). In addition to demonstrating the normal mucosal pattern of the oesophagus (Fig.1.4), a barium swallow may show a slight constriction approximately 2cm above the diaphragm, below which is an area of dilatation known as the vestibule, or phrenic ampulla (Fig.1.5). This area of dilatation should not be confused with the radiological appearances of a hiatus hernia. The oesophagus enters the stomach at an oblique angle just below the diaphragmatic crura approximately 40cm from the incisor teeth (Fig.1.6).

Food is transported from the pharynx to the stomach by the coordinated contraction of the muscular layers of the body of the

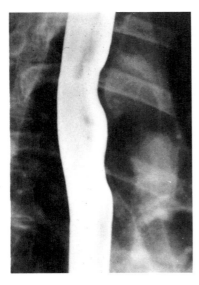

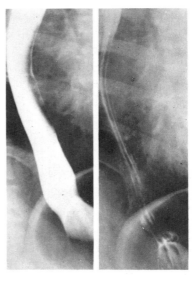

Fig.1.3 Barium swallow showing normal indentations due to the bronchus and aorta.

Fig.1.4 Barium swallow showing the pattern of oesophageal mucosa in the distended (left) and contracted (right) states. There are normally three to five parallel lines of barium lying within the crenated mucosal folds.

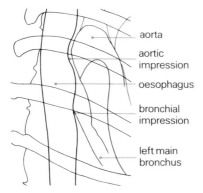

aorta

aortic impression

oesophagus

bronchial impression

left main bronchus

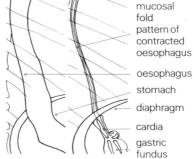

mucosal fold
pattern of contracted oesophagus

oesophagus

stomach

diaphragm

cardia

gastric fundus

oesophagus. This peristaltic contraction wave is relatively slow and moves down the oesophagus at a rate of 2-6cm sec^{-1}. When initiated by swallowing, it is known as primary peristalsis. Secondary peristalsis originates below the hypopharynx with no antecedent swallowing movement.

The barrier functions of the oesophagus are accomplished by the upper cricopharyngeus and lower oesophageal sphincters (LOS). The LOS is a zone of high pressure extending over the lower 3-4cm of the oesophagus with no definite anatomical counterpart. The normal resting LOS pressure is between 15 and 35mm Hg.

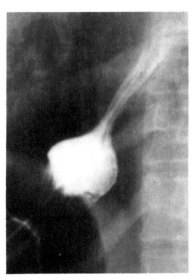

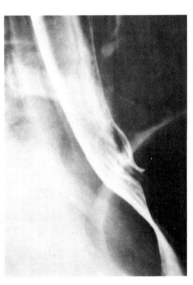

Fig.1.5 Barium swallow showing the phrenic ampulla at the lower end of the oesophagus.

Fig.1.6 Barium swallow showing the entry of the oesophagus into the fundus of the stomach, with barium cascading down the lesser gastric curve.

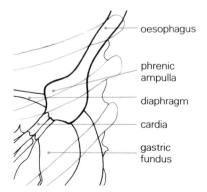

oesophagus

phrenic ampulla

diaphragm

cardia

gastric fundus

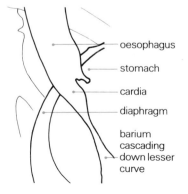

oesophagus

stomach

cardia

diaphragm

barium cascading down lesser curve

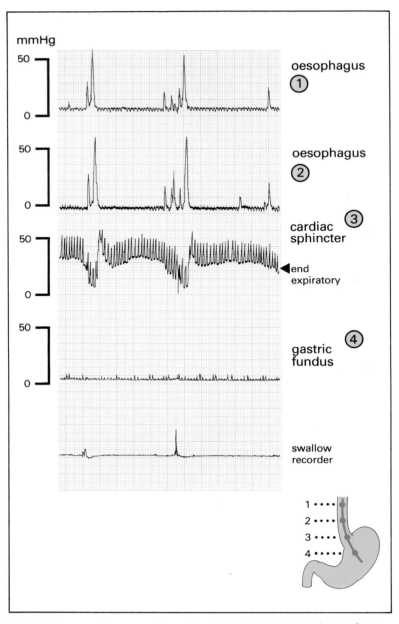

Fig.1.7 Manometric pressure trace from the body of the oesophagus, from the lower oesophageal sphincter and from the gastric fundus. Swallowing (bottom trace) is followed by progessive contractions of the oesophageal body and relaxation of the cardiac sphincter. Sphincter pressure trace shows marked respiratory excursions; positivity of these shows that the pressure is recorded from the subdiaphragmatic part of the cardiac sphincter.

A manometric pressure trace of normal peristalsis and sphincter relaxation shows that on swallowing the upper sphincter relaxes before passage of the bolus, after which it contracts. Swallowing is followed by a peristaltic contraction along the body of the oesophagus and the lower oesophageal sphincter relaxes just prior to the contraction wave reaching it, thus allowing passage of the bolus into the stomach (Fig.1.7).

The lower oesophageal sphincter alone is not sufficient to prevent gastro-oesophageal reflux and compression of the subdiaphragmatic portion of the oesophagus by a rise in intra-gastric or intra-abdominal pressure and the acute angle of entry of the oesophagus into the stomach are factors that help to prevent reflux.

The pH within the oesophagus is usually 5-7, unless there is a reflux of acid gastric contents. A pH recording from the lower oesophagus (Fig.1.8) may therefore show the presence of reflux and serial pH measurements can be used to determine the time taken for the oesophagus to be cleared of acid.

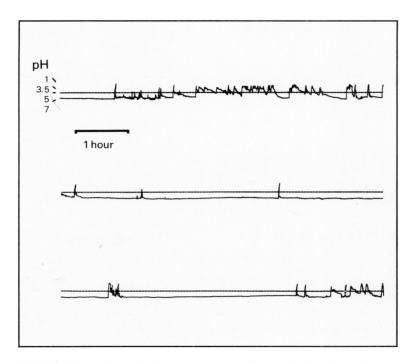

Fig.1.8 pH recording at the lower oesophagus demonstrating frequent episodes of reflux which lower the oesophageal pH below 3.5. Courtesy of Dr. J. Bennett.

Endoscopically the oesophageal body appears as a smooth featureless pink tube without prominent blood vessels (Fig.1.9). At the gastro-oesophageal junction transition from oesophageal to gastric mucosa is easily seen as an irregular circumferential line known as the ora serrata, gastric rosette or Z line (Fig.1.10). Histological examination of the oesophagus shows it to be lined by non-keratinised squamous epithelium.

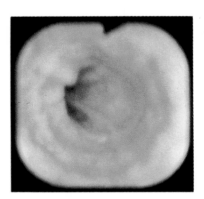

Fig.1.9 Endoscopic view of the oesophageal body showing pale pink squamous mucosa and distal deeper pink of the columnar, epithelial-lined gastric rosette.

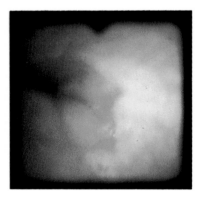

Fig.1.10 Endoscopic view of the oesophago-gastric junction showing sharp demarcation between the pale pink squamous epithelium of the oesophageal body and darker pink of the columnar gastric epithelium.

Papillae, extensions of the lamina propria, penetrate for a short distance into the epithelium. The lamina propria is separated from the underlying submucosa by a thin layer of smooth muscle, the muscularis mucosae. Deep to the submucosa is a circular and longitudinal muscle coat (Figs.1.11-1.13).

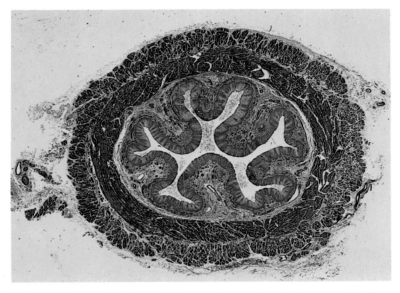

Fig.1.11 Cross-section through the oesophagus showing the convoluted lumen, squamous epithelial lining, the submucosa and the two outer layers of muscle. Trichrome stain, x 6. Courtesy of Dr. P. Wheater.

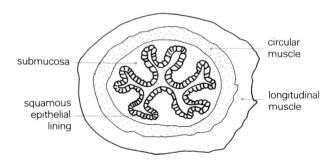

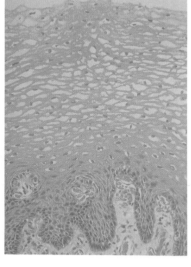

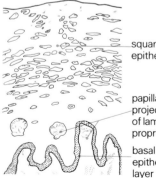

Fig. 1.12 Histology of a longitudinal section of the oesophagus. H & E stain, x 30. Courtesy of Dr. P. Wheater.

Fig.1.13 Histology of normal oesophageal squamous epithelium showing the shallow papillary projections of the lamina propria. H & E stain, x 140.

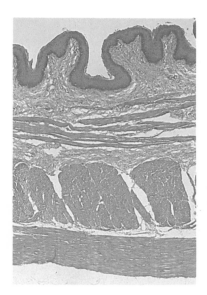

squamous epithelial lining

muscularis mucosae

submucosa

circular muscle

longitudinal muscle

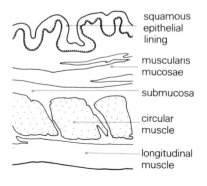

squamous epithelium

papillary projections of lamina propria

basal epithelial layer

Normal Stomach

The stomach connects the oesophagus to the duodenum (Figs. 1.14 & 1.15).

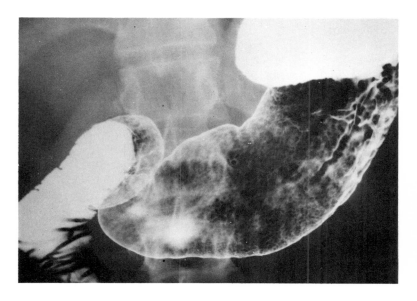

Fig.1.14 Barium meal (anteroposterior view) showing the normal anatomy of the stomach.

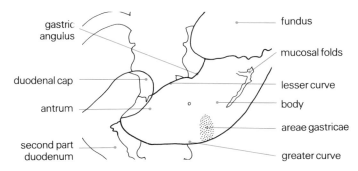

gastric angulus

duodenal cap

antrum

second part duodenum

fundus

mucosal folds

lesser curve

body

areae gastricae

greater curve

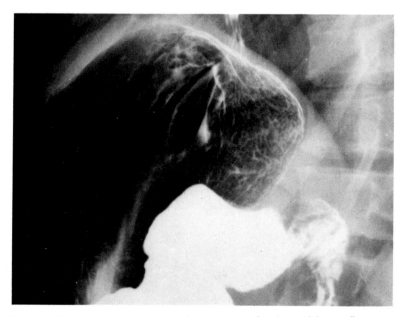

Fig.1.15 Barium meal (oblique view) showing the fundus and the cardia.

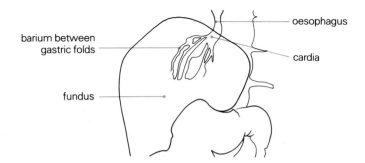

oesophagus

barium between gastric folds

cardia

fundus

Anatomically it is divided into several portions (Fig. 1.16).

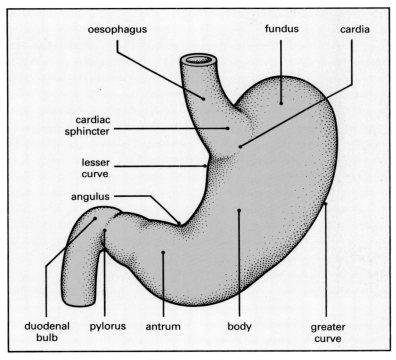

Fig.1.16 Diagram showing the normal anatomy of the stomach.

The cardia (Fig. 1.17) is situated just below the entrance of the oesophagus whilst the fundus of the stomach is that part which lies above the oesophago-gastric junction. The main part of the stomach is the body which has a shorter, lesser curve and longer, dependent greater curve (Fig. 1.18). The mucosa of the body of the stomach is thrown into folds known as rugae. The antrum represents approxi-

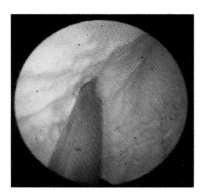

Fig. 1.17 The cardia viewed from below. Retroflexion of the endoscope shows the instrument entering through the cardia into the body of the stomach.

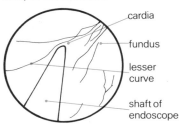

cardia

fundus

lesser
curve

shaft of
endoscope

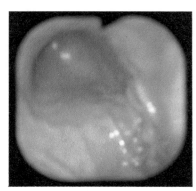

Fig. 1.18 Endoscopic view of the greater and lesser curves of the stomach.

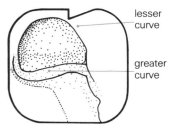

lesser
curve

greater
curve

mately the distal third of the stomach (Fig. 1.19). It is smooth with no rugae and is demarcated by the incisura angularis proximally (Fig. 1.20) and the pylorus distally. The exit from the stomach into the first part of the duodenum is the pylorus represented by a greatly thickened layer of circular muscle.

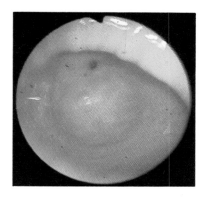

Fig. 1.19 Endoscopic view of the gastric antrum and pylorus.

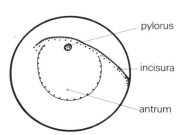

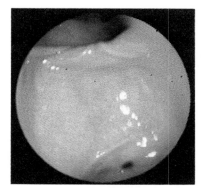

Fig. 1.20 Endoscopic view of the incisura with the instrument retroverted.

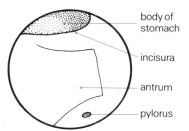

The stomach is innervated by parasympathetic nerves supplied by the vagus and sympathetic nerves which originate in the coeliac plexus. The vagus is divided into anterior and posterior trunks. The anterior trunk is further subdivided into an anterior gastric division that supplies the anterior wall of the stomach and a hepatic division that supplies the proximal duodenum (Fig. 1.21). Part of the posterior gastric division of the posterior vagal trunk supplies the posterior gastric wall. In addition to afferent fibres, the vagus contains 3 types of efferent fibre – cholinergic stimulatory, adrenergic inhibitory and non-adrenergic inhibitory. The cholinergic fibres play an important part in gastric secretion and motility.

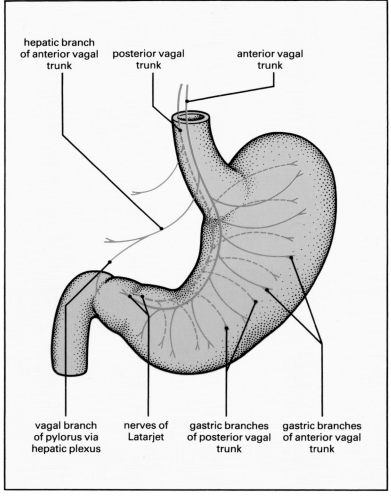

Fig.1.21 Diagram showing the anatomical arrangement of the vagus nerves.

The mucosa of the fundus and body of the stomach is covered by regular columnar epithelium which extends for a short distance into the gastric pits. The gastric glands open into the base of the pits. In the body the glands comprise two types of specialised secretory cells. In the upper half of the glands there are the parietal cells, which produce hydrochloric acid and intrinsic factor which binds vitamin B_{12}. In the lower half are found the pepsin-producing chief cells (Figs. 1.22-1.25).

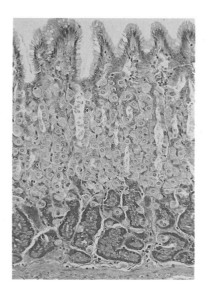

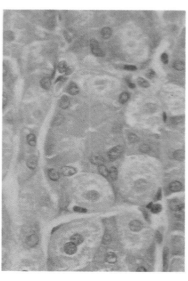

Fig. 1.22 Cross-section through the body of the stomach showing acid-secreting and pepsin-producing glands. H & E stain, x 50. Courtesy of Dr. P. Wheater.

Fig. 1.23 Histology of the body of the stomach showing the deep-staining pepsin-producing cells and the pale-staining parietal or acid secreting cells. H & E stain, x 480.

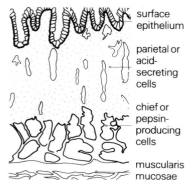

surface epithelium

parietal or acid-secreting cells

chief or pepsin-producing cells

muscularis mucosae

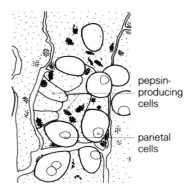

pepsin-producing cells

parietal cells

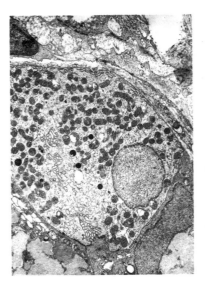

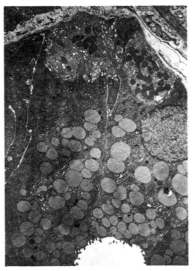

Fig.1.24 Electron micrograph of an acid-secreting or parietal cell showing abundant mitochondria and the intra-cytoplasmic canalicular system of the cell. x 3000. Courtesy of Dr. D. Day.

Fig. 1.25 Electron micrograph showing the typical granules of a chief or pepsin-producing cell from the body of the stomach. ×3000. Courtesy of Dr. D. Day.

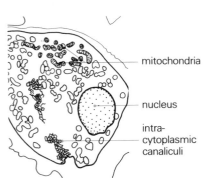

mitochondria

nucleus

intra-cytoplasmic canaliculi

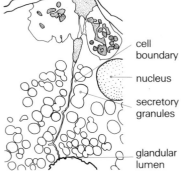

cell boundary

nucleus

secretory granules

glandular lumen

The antral, or pyloric glands do not contain acid or pepsin-producing cells, but are mucus-secreting (Figs. 1.26 & 1.27).

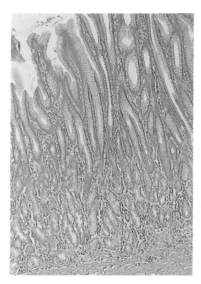

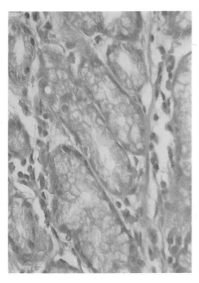

Fig.1.26 Cross-section through the pyloric region of the stomach showing the deeper gastric pits compared to those in the body which open into the mucus-secreting pyloric glands beneath. H & E stain, x 50.

Fig.1.27 The simple mucus-secreting glands in the pylorus. H & E stain, x 125.

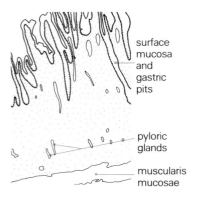

surface mucosa and gastric pits

pyloric glands

muscularis mucosae

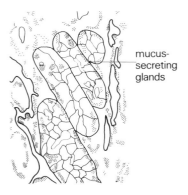

mucus-secreting glands

The majority of the gastrin-producing, or 'G' cells, are found in the antrum interspersed between these mucus cells (Figs. 1.28-1.30).

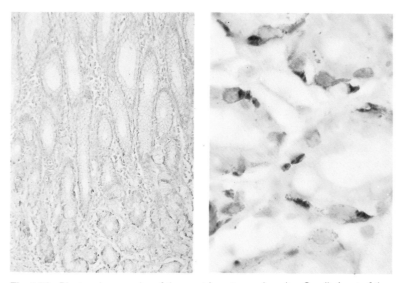

Fig.1.28 Photomicrographs of the gastric antrum showing G cells (part of the APUD system) within the pyloric glands. Grimelius, silver impregnation, x 120 (left), x 800 (right).

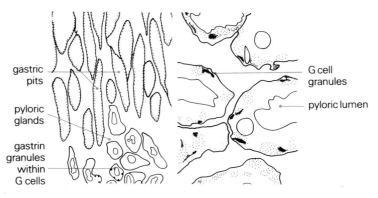

gastric pits

pyloric glands

gastrin granules within G cells

G cell granules

pyloric lumen

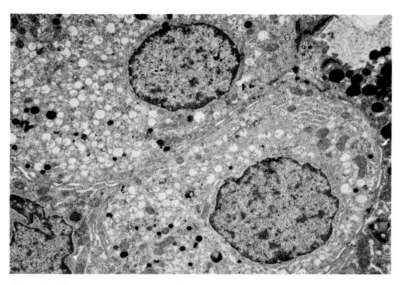

Fig.1.29 Electron micrograph of G cells demonstrating the two patterns (dense and clear) of gastrin neurosecretory granules, x 7500. Courtesy of Dr. J. Polak.

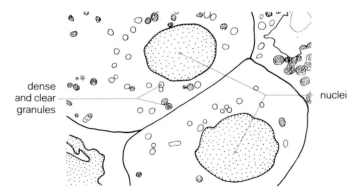

dense and clear granules

nuclei

The stomach functions as a reservoir and mixing chamber for ingested food allowing gastric acid and pepsin to start the process of digestion. The volume of the resting stomach is 50ml or less. However, receptive relaxation of the gastric body occurs as food and liquid are ingested so that there is little rise in intra-gastric pressure.

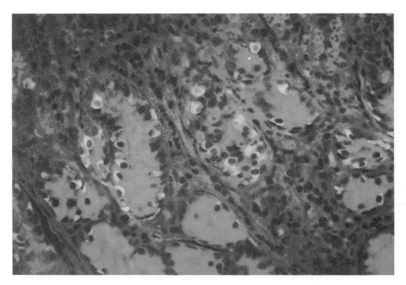

Fig. 1.30 Green fluorescing G cells in the pyloric glands demonstrated by using fluorescine-labelled anti-gastrin. The pyloric glands appear brown with the mucin (red) which has taken up the PAS (periodic – Schiff reagent) counterstain. Courtesy of Dr. J. Polak.

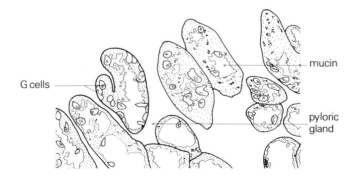

The mucosa of the stomach is protected by a layer of mucus, a gelatinous material composed of proteins, glycoproteins and mucopolysaccharides secreted by the surface epithelium (Figs.1.31 & 1.32). The functions of mucus remain unclear. It appears to protect the gastric mucosa against surface injury by physical irritants and to buffer gastric acid under basal conditions, although its effect in buffering stimulated acid secretion is negligible.

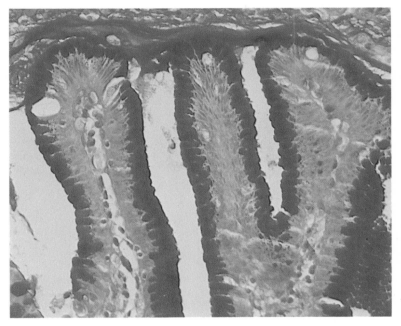

Fig.1.31 Histology of the surface gastric mucosa showing the covering layer of mucin. H & E stain, x 320.

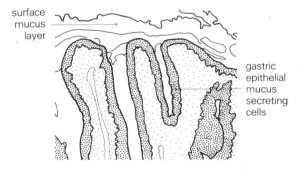

surface mucus layer

gastric epithelial mucus secreting cells

The most important physiological mediators of gastric acid secretion are acetylcholine, gastrin and histamine. The vagus nerve acts on the parietal cells to stimulate acid production and on the antral gastrin cells to stimulate gastrin release, in both cases via the action of acetylcholine. In addition, acetylcholine potentiates the parietal cell response to other secretagogues. Gastrin is also released directly by the chemical action of peptides and amino acids bathing the pyloric glandular mucosa and by antral distension.

The parietal cells also contain histamine receptors, and histamine,

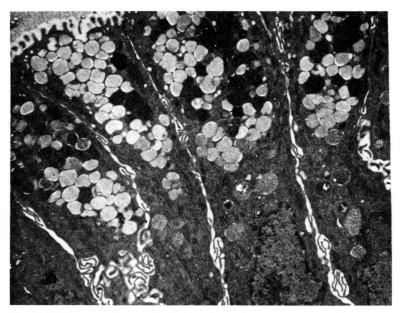

Fig.1.32 Electron micrograph showing the surface, mucus-secreting epithelial cells of the stomach. x 3200.

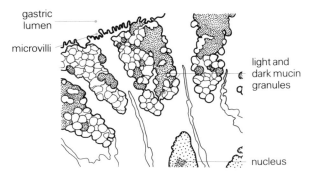

which occurs throughout the entire gastro-intestinal tract, also stimulates acid production. It is not clear whether histamine is the final common path for gastric secretion, or whether receptors for histamine, gastrin and acetylcholine on the parietal cells interact with each other and with the secretory apparatus within the cell. Both the injection of histamine and the synthetic analogue of gastrin, pentagastrin, are capable of maximally stimulating acid production by the parietal cells. This is the basis of the augmented histamine and pentagastrin tests for assessment of acid secretory capacity (Fig. 1.33).

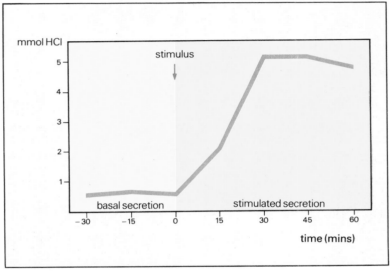

Fig.1.33 Acid secretion study showing increased gastric acid output following stimulation with pentagastrin, $6mgKg^{-1}$

Peristaltic waves (Figs. 1.34 & 1.35) initiated by the gastric pacemaker in the fundus of the stomach occur at a rate of 3 min^{-1} and these gradually propel the viscous gastric contents into the distal antrum.

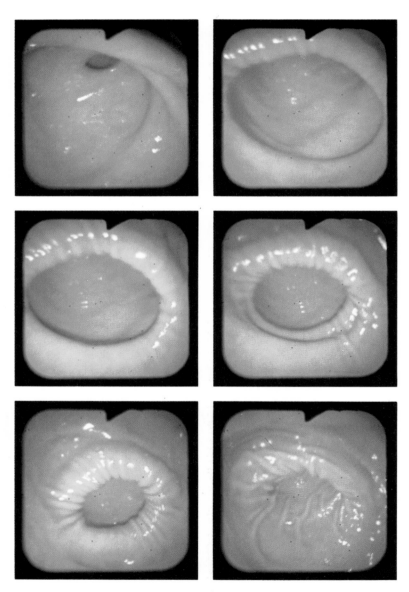

Fig.1.34 Sequential endoscopic views showing a peristaltic contraction wave advancing along the body of the stomach to the antrum and terminating in closing the pylorus.

The rate at which the contents pass into the duodenum depends upon their physical and chemical composition: solids, lipids and hypertonic fluids all empty at a slower rate than isotonic fluids.

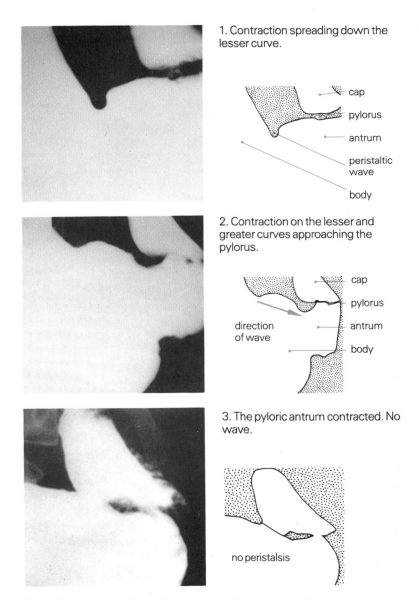

1. Contraction spreading down the lesser curve.

cap
pylorus
antrum
peristaltic wave
body

2. Contraction on the lesser and greater curves approaching the pylorus.

cap
pylorus
direction of wave
antrum
body

3. The pyloric antrum contracted. No wave.

no peristalsis

Fig.1.35 Series of radiographs with the patient prone and barium in the stomach illustrating a peristaltic contraction wave.

Receptors in the duodenal mucosa respond to the chemical composition of duodenal contents to regulate, by negative feedback, the rate at which stomach emptying occurs. As pressure rises in the antrum a small fraction of the antral contents pass through the open pylorus into the duodenum. The pylorus then abruptly contracts causing antral pressure to increase and thus propel contents back into the body of the stomach. Unlike the cardia, in the resting state, the pylorus is always open and only closes during peristalsis (Fig.1.36). This antral 'pump' therefore mixes gastric contents and digestive juices and finely regulates the rate of gastric emptying (Fig.1.37).

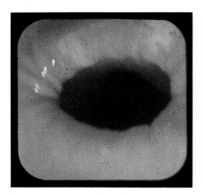 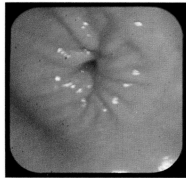

Fig.1.36 Endoscopic views of the pylorus open and closed.

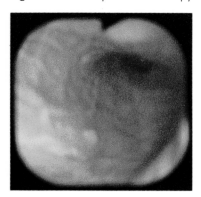

Fig.1.37 Endoscopic view of a pool of gastric juice.

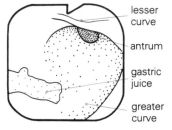

2.
Oesophageal Disease

Gastro-oesophageal Reflux

The reflux of gastric or intestinal contents into the oesophagus may cause the symptoms of heartburn (pyrosis), oesophagitis, strictures, ulceration or less commonly, replacement of the normal squamous epithelium of the oesophagus by columnar epithelium (Barrett's syndrome). Gastro-oesophageal reflux can occur with or without a hiatus hernia, in pregnancy, in systemic sclerosis, following surgery (eg. for achalasia), and with certain pharmacological agents, or after smoking.

The aetiology of reflux remains controversial although the common

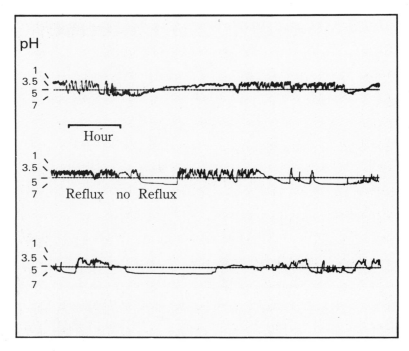

Fig.2.1 pH recording from the lower oesophagus demonstrating frequent falls in pH due to episodes of reflux. Courtesy of Dr. J. R. Bennett.

factor in all the above situations is a decreased resting lower oesophageal sphincter pressure. Normal sphincteric pressure is 15-30mm Hg, but in patients with reflux it is usually 10mm Hg or lower. Gastro-oesophageal reflux can be demonstrated by means of a pH probe: a decrease of pH from 6 to 2 signifies an episode of reflux (Fig. 2.1). In routine clinical practice reflux may be demonstrated radiologically during a barium swallow (Fig. 2.2) although this does not always correlate with symptoms, for example, heartburn and regurgitation.

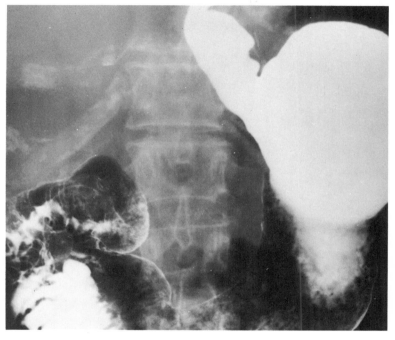

Fig.2.2 Barium swallow (supine view) showing spontaneous gastro-oesophageal reflux.

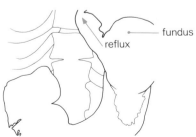

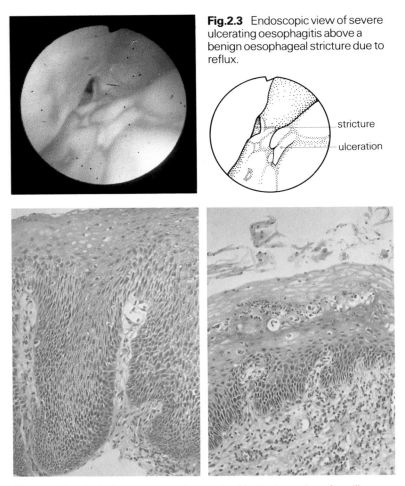

Fig.2.3 Endoscopic view of severe ulcerating oesophagitis above a benign oesophageal stricture due to reflux.

stricture

ulceration

Fig.2.4 Histological appearance of oesophagitis. Prolongation of papillae extending two thirds of the way through the squamous epithelium towards the surface (left, x 340). This is a feature of mild oesophagitis. Oesophageal mucosa showing moderate oesophagitis (middle, x 130). Inflammatory cells

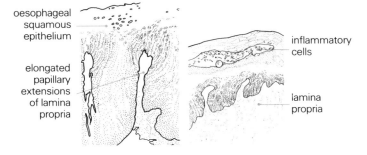

oesophageal squamous epithelium

elongated papillary extensions of lamina propria

inflammatory cells

lamina propria

Oesophagitis

Oesophagitis can be graded as mild, moderate or severe; although the endoscopic and histological degree of severity does not correlate well with symptoms of reflux eg. heartburn (Figs.2.3 & 2.4). Rarely, oesophagitis may be caused by drugs (Fig.2.5).

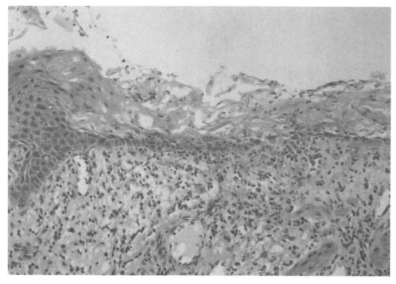

(polymorphs) are seen within the mucosa and beneath it. In severe oesophagitis the surface squamous epithelium becomes ulcerated with an infiltrate of inflammatory cells present in the lamina propria (right, x130). H & E stains.

ulcerated squamous epithelium

inflammatory infiltrate in lamina propria

Stricture

Prolonged and severe reflux may lead to fibrosis and stricture formation, accompanied by progressive dysphagia, initially for solids

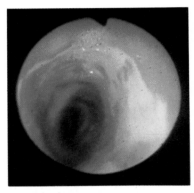

Fig.2.5 Endoscopic view of severe haemorrhagic oesophagitis with bleeding and ulceration following ingestion of emepronium bromide (upper). Barium swallow from the same patient demonstrates irregularity and ulceration (lower). Courtesy of Dr. R. Tobias.

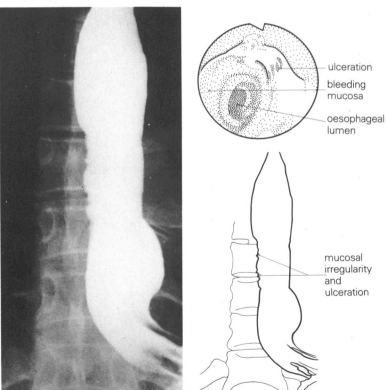

ulceration

bleeding mucosa

oesophageal lumen

mucosal irregularity and ulceration

and later for liquids. Whilst the radiological interpretation of a stricture as benign (Fig. 2.6) is usually correct, particularly when it occurs above a hiatus hernia (Fig. 2.7), radiological criteria are not sufficiently precise

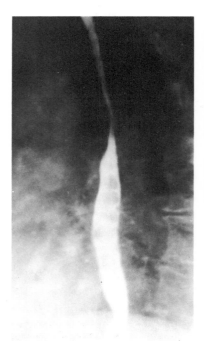

Fig.2.6 Barium swallow showing a smooth stricture in the mid-oesophagus. Negative biopsies and cytology from the stricture confirmed its benign nature.

Fig.2.7 Barium swallow showing a sliding hiatus hernia with a short stricture above it.

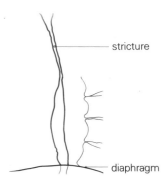

stricture

diaphragm

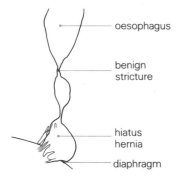

oesophagus

benign stricture

hiatus hernia

diaphragm

to exclude malignancy. Endoscopy (Fig. 2.8) with multiple biopsies and brush exfoliative cytology is therefore mandatory following the radiological demonstration of a stricture. Benign oesophageal strictures may follow suicidal ingestion of caustic soda, or other corrosive agents. In such cases the strictures are frequently multiple and severe (Fig. 2.9).

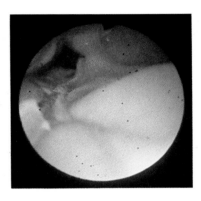

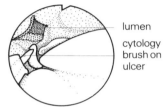

Fig.2.8 Endoscopic view in severe oesophagitis due to reflux with shallow ulceration and surrounding hyperaemia. Brush cytology is being taken from an ulcerated area.

lumen

cytology brush on ulcer

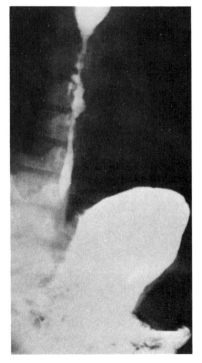

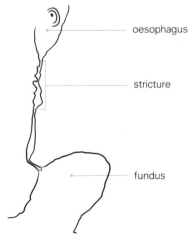

Fig.2.9 Barium swallow showing stricturing in the lower oesophagus following ingestion of caustic soda.

oesophagus

stricture

fundus

Oesophageal Ulcer

Many patients with severe reflux oesophagitis have superficial mucosal ulceration (Fig. 2.10) but only a minority will develop a deeper ulcer involving the muscle layers of the oesophagus (Fig. 2.11).

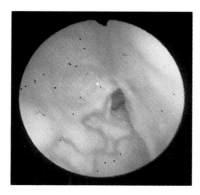

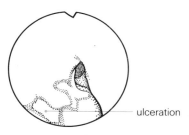

Fig.2.10 Endoscopic appearance of superficial oesophageal ulceration due to reflux.

ulceration

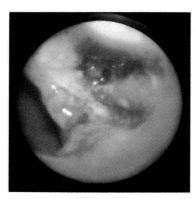

Fig.2.11 Endoscopic appearance of a deep distal oesophageal ulcer.

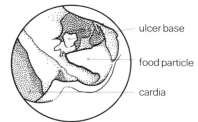

ulcer base

food particle

cardia

Rarely the ulcer may perforate, or give rise to a haematemesis. Such ulcers are usually seen radiologically as a projection of contrast outside the lumen (Fig. 2.12).

Barrett's Syndrome

A further uncommon complication of longstanding reflux is the replacement of the normal squamous epithelium of the oesophageal mucosa by areas of columnar epithelium. On endoscopy the normal mucosa of the oesophagus is replaced by reddish areas of discoloration

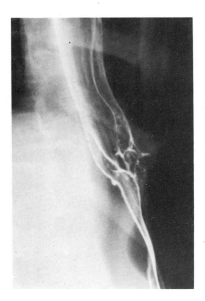

Fig.2.12 Barium swallow in severe reflux oesophagitis with several ulcers in the distal oesophagus.

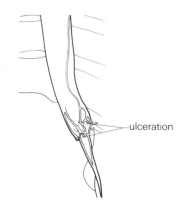

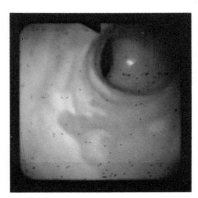

Fig.2.13 Endoscopic view of Barrett's mucosa showing areas of deeper pink columnar epithelium amongst the pale pink, normal, squamous oesophageal mucosa.

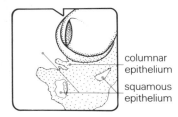

resembling gastric mucosa (Fig. 2.13).

Histologically, beside the presence of columnar epithelium, acid-secreting cells and villiform epithelium of intestinal pattern may be present (Fig. 2.14).

Barrett's syndrome is particularly likely to occur in patients with severe and continuous reflux. The main clinical importance of this metaplastic change is its premalignant potential: an adenocarcinoma may develop in up to 10% of patients.

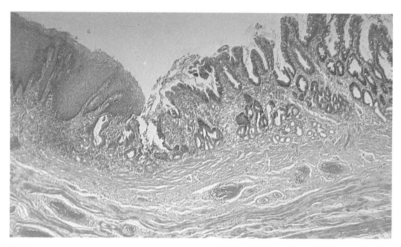

Fig.2.14 Histological appearance of the oesophagus in Barrett's syndrome. The features are replacement of part of the normal squamous epithelium of the oesophagus by villiform intestinal type columnar epithelium along with underlying crypts and pyloric-pattern glands. H & E stain, x 30.

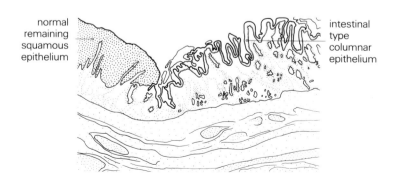

normal remaining squamous epithelium

intestinal type columnar epithelium

Diverticula

Oesophageal diverticula are pouches lined with one or more layers of the oesophageal wall. They may occur immediately above the upper oesophageal sphincter (Zenker's diverticulum, or pharyngeal pouch), near the mid-point of the oesophagus, or immediately above the lower oesophageal sphincter (epiphrenic diverticulum). The aetiology of these diverticula is not clear, although abnormal motility and incoordination of sphincter relaxation may cause diverticula at the upper and lower ends of the oesophagus; these are therefore called

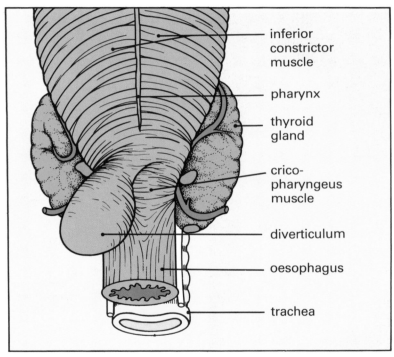

inferior constrictor muscle

pharynx

thyroid gland

crico-pharyngeus muscle

diverticulum

oesophagus

trachea

Fig.2.15 Diagram of a pharyngeal pouch protruding between the oblique fibres of the inferior pharyngeal constrictor and transverse cricopharyngeus muscle.

pulsion diverticula. Mid-oesophageal diverticula, however, are usually due to traction from inflammatory adhesions within the mediastinum, most commonly following tuberculosis.

A pharyngeal pouch (Zenker's diverticulum) is not a true diverticulum because its walls consist of only the mucosa prolapsing through the cricopharyngeus muscle (Fig. 2.15). It is however, the most important of the oesophageal diverticula, because it may be large enough to obstruct the oesophageal lumen producing dysphagia (Fig. 2.16), while aspiration of its contents can lead to respiratory complications.

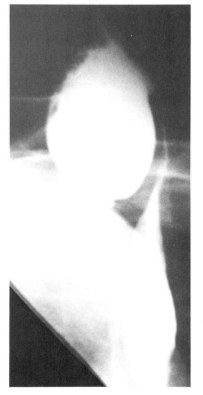

Fig. 2.16 A large cricopharyngeal pouch filled with barium. The pouch compresses the oesophagus causing dysphagia.

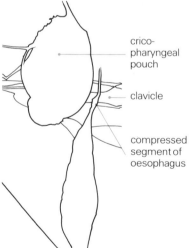

crico-
pharyngeal
pouch

clavicle

compressed
segment of
oesophagus

By contrast, mid-oesophageal diverticula (Fig.2.17), are frequently asymptomatic, whilst symptoms from an epiphrenic diverti-

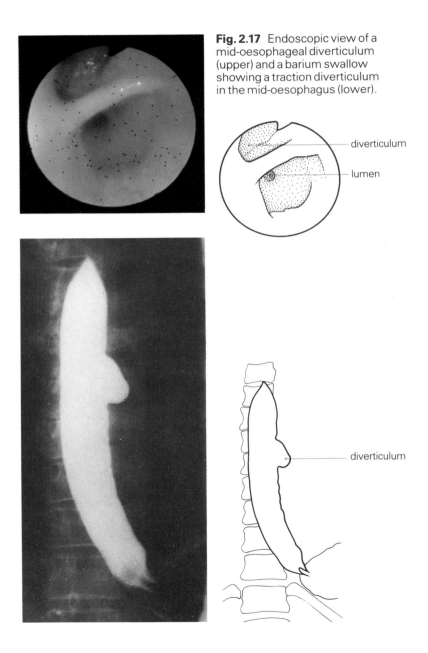

Fig. 2.17 Endoscopic view of a mid-oesophageal diverticulum (upper) and a barium swallow showing a traction diverticulum in the mid-oesophagus (lower).

diverticulum

lumen

diverticulum

culum (Fig.2.18) are thought to be related to the associated motor abnormalities, rather than to the presence of the diverticulum itself.

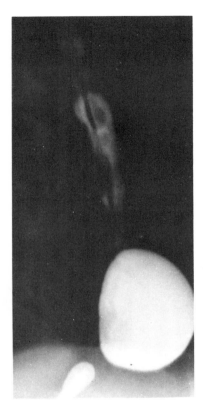

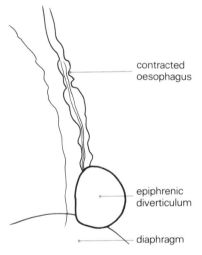

Fig.2.18 Barium swallow showing an epiphrenic diverticulum. The oesophagus is contracted and the large epiphrenic diverticulum has filled with barium. Courtesy of Dr. H. Shawdon.

contracted oesophagus

epiphrenic diverticulum

diaphragm

Oesophageal Carcinoma

Ninety-five per cent or more of oesophageal carcinomas are of the squamous cell type. Patients present initially with dysphagia for solids and later for liquids as the tumour progresses. Weight loss, anorexia and occasionally pain or haematemesis are accompanying symptoms. The tumours arise in the upper, middle or lower third of the oesophagus. Radiologically they appear as an asymmetrical diffuse thickening of the oesophageal wall (Fig.2.19), a polypoid intrusion into the oesophageal lumen (Fig.2.20), or as a stricture which characteristically has a shouldered appearance (Fig.2.21), unlike the more tapering benign strictures.

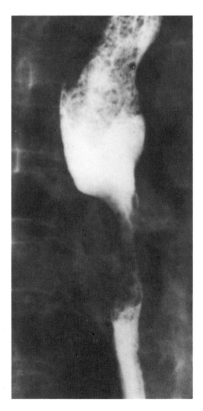

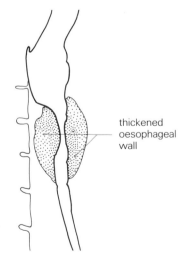

Fig.2.19 Barium swallow showing irregular stricturing in the lower oesophagus due to a carcinoma. The oesophageal wall is thickened by the tumour.

thickened oesophageal wall

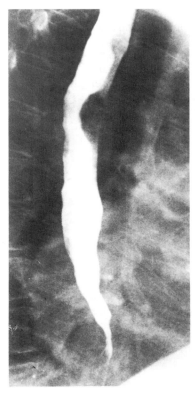

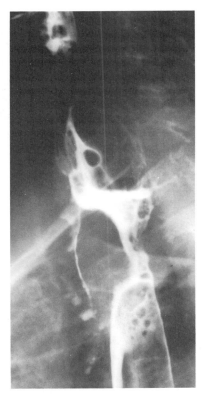

Fig.2.20 Barium swallow showing a polypoid carcinoma in the distal oesophagus.

Fig.2.21 Barium swallow showing an annular carcinoma in the upper oesophagus with polypoid mucosal thickening and shouldering.

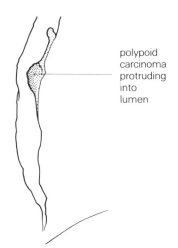

polypoid carcinoma protruding into lumen

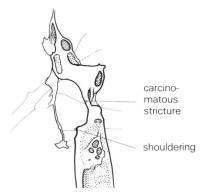

carcino-matous stricture

shouldering

Endoscopic appearances reflect the radiological findings (Fig. 2.22), and biopsy and cytology are necessary to establish the diagnosis.

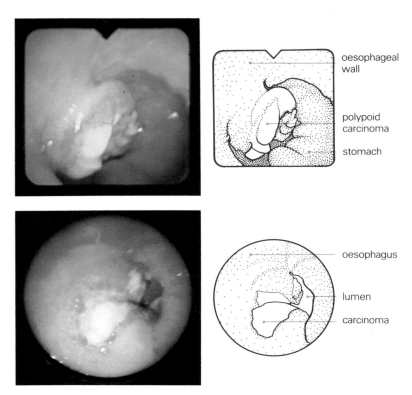

oesophageal wall

polypoid carcinoma

stomach

oesophagus

lumen

carcinoma

Fig.2.22 Endoscopic view of polypoid carcinomata in the distal oesophagus (upper). Gastric mucosa is seen distal to the carcinoma in this patient who presented with dysphagia. The squamous cell circinoma (lower) obstructed the distal oesophagus producing a stricture. Courtesy of Dr. F. Silverstein.

Macroscopically the tumours can be classified as fungating, ulcerative or infiltrative (Fig.2.23). By the time the diagnosis is made they are usually large. Histology of the resected specimen shows islands of malignant squamous epithelium penetrating the oesophageal wall. In patients who complain of dysphagia only, mucosal irregularity is occasionally seen endoscopically. The biopsy however, may show *in*

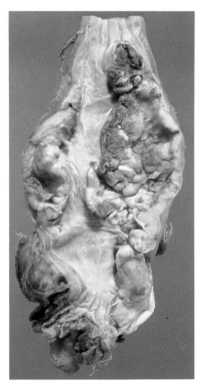

Fig.2.23 A large, nodular, partly ulcerated tumour extending over the middle third of the oesophagus. Courtesy of Dr. A. Pomerance.

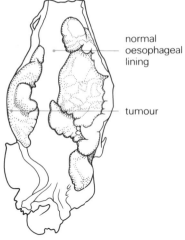

normal oesophageal lining

tumour

situ cancer, a situation comparable to early gastric cancer (Fig. 2.24).

True adenocarcinomas of the oesophagus are rare, and probably account for only three to five per cent of oesophageal malignancies if adenocarcinomas of the gastro-oesophageal junction are excluded. Those in the proximal two-thirds arise from congenital aberrant gastric mucosa, or submucosal glands. Those in the distal third probably arise

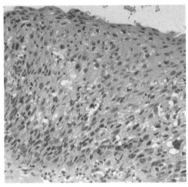

Fig.2.24 Histological appearances of oesophageal carcinoma. The *in situ* appearance shows full thickness nuclear atypicality but no invasion (upper, x 350).

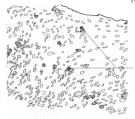

irregular pleomorphic nuclei throughout mucosa

An early invasive squamous carcinoma with downgrowth of malignant epithelium encroaching into the submucosa (middle, x 55).

malignant epithelium extending into wall

An established, infiltrating, well differentiated, squamous carcinoma (lower, x 80). Islands of malignant epithelium are invading deep into the oesophageal muscle. H & E stain.

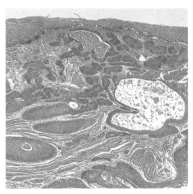

islands of malignant epithelium penetrating wall

muscle coat

from the metaplastic columnar epithelium that occurs in Barrett's syndrome.

Adenocarcinomas of the gastric fundus often grow upward and invade the oesophagus producing symptoms of an oesophageal tumour (Fig. 2.25).

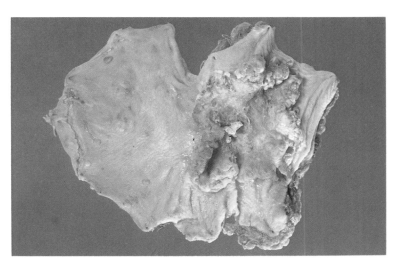

Fig.2.25 Macroscopic appearance of an ulcerating adenocarcinoma at the gastro-oesophageal junction. It is impossible to distinguish a true junctional carcinoma from one arising in the fundus and growing upwards to involve the distal oesophagus.

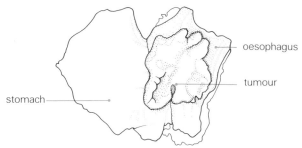

Careful radiological examination may show the carcinoma in the fundus (Fig.2.26) whilst at endoscopy retroflexion of the instrument after it has been passed into the stomach may also demonstrate the tumour (Fig.2.27).

Macroscopically the patterns are similar to those of the squamous

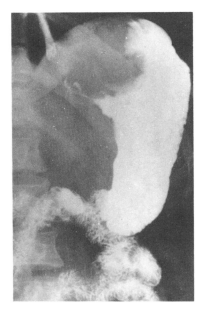

Fig.2.26 Barium swallow showing a large fundal carcinoma. Courtesy of Dr. H. Shawdon.

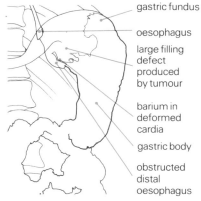

gastric fundus

oesophagus

large filling defect produced by tumour

barium in deformed cardia

gastric body

obstructed distal oesophagus

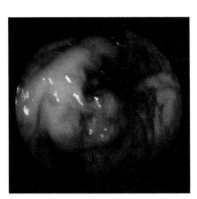

Fig.2.27 Endoscopic view of adenocarcinoma at the cardia which could only be seen with the instrument retroflexed. Courtesy of Dr. F. Silverstein.

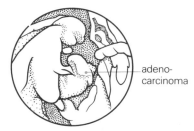

adeno-carcinoma

cell carcinomas already described. Histologically, malignant glandular tissue is obvious, often invading upwards under the overlying oesophageal squamous lining (Fig. 2.28).

Dysphagia may also be produced by extrinsic compression of the oesophagus by tumours or aortic aneurysms (Fig. 2.29).

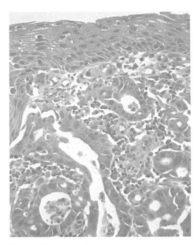

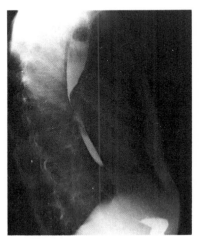

Fig.2.28 Histological appearance of an infiltrating adenocarcinoma extending upward from the stomach. H & E stain, x 40.

Fig.2.29 Barium swallow showing extrinsic compression of the oesophagus by malignant mediastinal lymph nodes in a patient with a carcinoma of the bronchus.

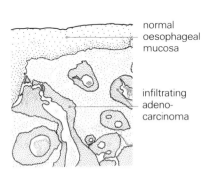

normal oesophageal mucosa

infiltrating adeno- carcinoma

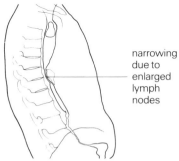

narrowing due to enlarged lymph nodes

Rings and Webs

Oesophageal webs are thin membranes of connective tissue covered by normal squamous epithelium. Although they may occur anywhere along the oesophagus, they are usually situated in the upper third and are frequently asymmetrical (Fig. 2.30). The association of a cervical oeso-phageal web and iron deficiency anaemia in predominantly middle-aged women is known as the Plummer-Vinson, or Paterson-Kelly syndrome. Such patients may also have leukoplakia of the oro-pharynx (Fig. 2.31) and koilonychia. These webs regress sponta-neously with treatment of the iron deficiency anaemia. Although webs of the cervical oesophagus do not show aberrant epithelial changes, the Plummer-Vinson syndrome is associated with an increased inci-dence of post-cricoid carcinoma.

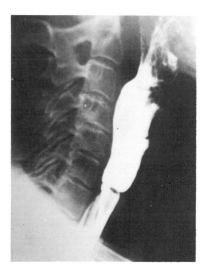

Fig. 2.30 Barium swallow showing a clearly defined web arising from the anterior wall of the oesophagus and partly encircling it. A jet of barium is passing through the narrowed lumen at the level of the web.

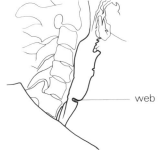

web

Fig. 2.31 White thickened plaque of leukoplakia on the labial mucosa. Courtesy of Dr. S. Goolamali.

Two types of oesophageal ring have been described. The lower oesophageal, or Schatzki ring is a symmetrical submucosal fibrous thickening that occurs at the lower end of the oesophagus at the squamo-columnar junction and measures approximately 1-3mm in thickness (Fig.2.32). The ring can be seen endoscopically above the diaphragmatic indentation (Fig.2.33). The other type of ring is thought to be muscular and occurs just cephalad to the site of the Schatzki ring, at the junction of the distal oesophagus and the uppermost part of the lower oesophageal sphincter. Manometrically, the muscular ring corresponds to a high pressure zone and is frequently associated with oesophageal motor disorders and diffuse oesophageal spasm. Both webs and rings cause intermittent dysphagia for solids. Occasionally bolus impaction may occur.

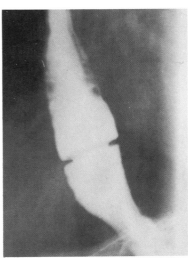

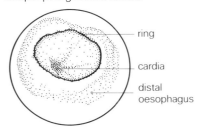

Fig.2.32 Barium swallow showing a narrow ring in the lower oesophagus. This is atypical of the appearance of a Schatzki ring. The ring is often visible only when the oesophagus is fully distended by barium. Courtesy of Dr. H. Shawdon.

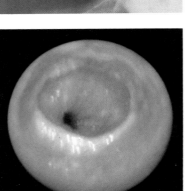

Fig.2.33 Endoscopic view of a Schatzki ring situated at the junction of the pale pink oesophageal and deeper pink gastric mucosa.

Achalasia of the Cardia

Achalasia is an uncommon disorder of oesophageal motility of unknown aetiology. The clinical and pathological features may be mimicked by infection with *Trypanosoma cruzi* in residents of South America (Chagas' disease).

There is a defect of oesophageal motility with lack of peristalsis in the distal two thirds of the gullet and an incomplete, or absent relaxation of the lower oesophageal sphincter in response to a voluntary swallow. In some cases the resting lower oesophageal sphincter pressure is abnormally high. These abnormalities lead to a progressive dilatation of the oesophagus above the lower oesophageal sphincter (Fig.2.34). In severe cases a chest radiograph may show a widened mediastinum with an air-fluid level due to the food and secretions which accumulate with-

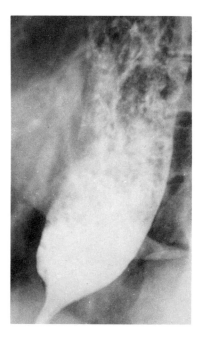

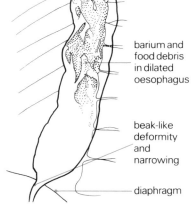

Fig.2.34 Barium swallow showing achalasia with dilatation of the oesophagus. Barium is mixing with food residue in the oesophagus. The oesophagus narrows to a typical beak-like deformity at the level of the cardia.

barium and food debris in dilated oesophagus

beak-like deformity and narrowing

diaphragm

in the grossly dilated oesophagus (Fig. 2.35). Oesophageal manometry demonstrates absent peristalsis in the body of the gullet, the normal progressive muscle activity being replaced by absent or weak synchronous contractions and an increased resting lower oesophageal sphincter pressure. Patients generally present with dysphagia for both liquids and solids, although in up to a third of patients chest pain may be prominent, particularly in the early stage of the disease. Regurgitation of oesophageal contents may lead to recurrent aspiration pneumonia bronchiectasis and lung abscesses.

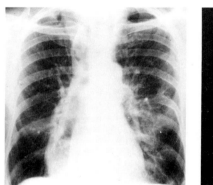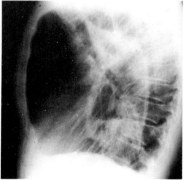

Fig.2.35 Radiograph showing a widened right mediastinal border due to the dilated oesophagus (left). A fluid level is seen in the lower part. A lateral view shows the air-fluid level in the dilated oesophagus (right). The height of the fluid level will vary according to the volume of food residue in the oesophagus. These changes are only seen in gross achalasia.

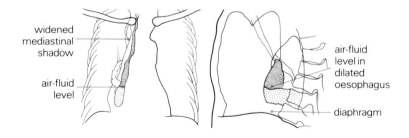

Macroscopically, in parallel with the radiological findings, the oesophagus is grossly dilated above a narrow distal segment (Fig.2.36). Special staining techniques are required to demonstrate the microscopic abnormality, which is a loss of ganglion cells in the myenteric plexus. Here two types of ganglion cells are normally present, argyrophilic and non-argyrophilic: the latter are decreased in number in achalasia especially in the dilated portion of the oesophagus.

In addition to the respiratory complications of the disorder, there is an increased risk of developing a squamous carcinoma within the dilated segment. This condition can be confused with an infiltrating adenocarcinoma of the gastric fundus mimicking the radiological and endoscopic features of achalasia.

Diffuse Spasm

Diffuse spasm is a disorder of oesophageal motility characterised clinically by episodic dysphagia and by chest pain resembling angina pectoris. The symptoms may occur without warning, although frequently they are provoked by deglutition and less commonly by the ingestion of hot or cold liquids. In its severe form diffuse oesophageal spasm causes the radiological appearances on barium swallow of

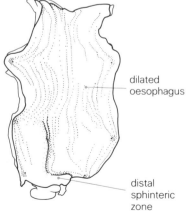

Fig.2.36 Macroscopic appearance of the oesophagus in achalasia showing massive proximal dilatation above the distal sphincteric zone. Courtesy of Dr. D. Lovell.

dilated oesophagus

distal sphincteric zone

tertiary contractions, or a 'corkscrew' oesophagus with pseudo-diverticula (Fig. 2.37). Less severe cases can only be demonstrated by manometry, which may show disordered motility within the lower two thirds of the oesophagus with repetitive, spontaneous, non-peristaltic contractions (Fig. 2.38). Manometry often suggests that the pressure within the body of the oesophagus is increased due to the

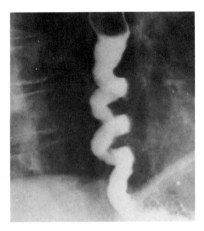

Fig.2.37 Barium swallow showing diffuse oesophageal spasm with a typical 'corkscrew' deformity.

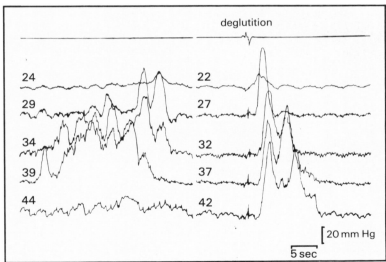

Fig.2.38 Manometric record showing excessive and uncoordinated oesophageal contractions in diffuse spasm. The top trace records swallows. Numbers on the other traces show the distance in cm from the incisor teeth. Courtesy of Prof. G. Van Trappen.

frequent contractions. It may also show an increased resting lower oesophageal sphincter pressure, although unlike in achalasia, relaxation of the sphincter during swallowing is normal.

Secondary diffuse spasm may occasionally occur when there is distal obstruction such as a tumour, or with gastro-oesophageal reflux, and these conditions must be excluded in any patient who initially appears to have the primary form of the disorder.

Systemic Sclerosis (Scleroderma)

Patients with either systemic sclerosis (Fig. 2.39) or with the mixed connective tissue disease syndrome frequently have pronounced

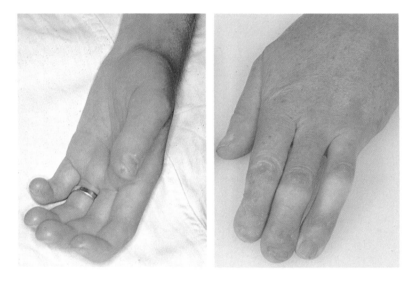

Fig.2.39 The hand in scleroderma showing shiny tethered skin, pulp atrophy, pitting scars, digital ulceration and flexion contractures (left), and another case showing in addition, Raynaud's phenomenon (right). The fifth finger was amputated for gangrene. Courtesy of Dr. C. Black.

oesophageal motor dysfunction due to destruction of smooth muscle. Abnormal motility comprises diminished, or absent peristalsis in the distal two thirds of the oesophagus and decreased lower oesophageal sphincter pressure. These changes can occur before any other systemic manifestation of the disease, and then manometry is helpful in distinguishing the condition from achalasia (Fig. 2.40). Radiologically, there is absent peristalsis and dilatation of the oesophagus with free gastro-oesophageal reflux, which in advanced cases may result in severe oesophagitis and stricture formation.

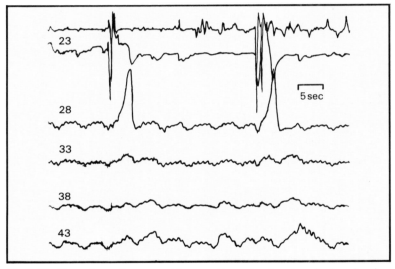

Fig.2.40 Oesophageal manometric record in systemic sclerosis showing the absence of oesophageal peristalsis in the lower part of the gullet (smooth muscle). Numbers on tracings refer to the distance in cm from incisor teeth. The top trace records swallows. Courtesy of Prof. G. Van Trappen.

About sixty per cent of patients complain of dysphagia although in others reflux symptoms predominate. Similar abnormalities of motility and sphincter function can occur in other collagen vascular disorders, or in patients with Raynaud's disease in whom there are no other cutaneous manifestations of systemic sclerosis.

Histologically there is a progressive atrophy of the smooth muscle coat. It is replaced by fibrous tissue which also involves the submucosa (Fig.2.41). However, there is marked variation and either muscular, or submucosal changes may predominate. Involved arteries and arterioles show a characteristic mucoid intimal thickening.

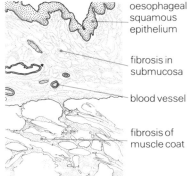

Fig.2.41 Histological appearance in scleroderma showing increased fibrosis of the submucosa (blue) fragmenting the muscularis and beginning to disrupt the main muscle coat. Martius Scarlet Blue stain, x 20.

oesophageal squamous epithelium

fibrosis in submucosa

blood vessel

fibrosis of muscle coat

Foreign Bodies

Foreign bodies can become impacted in the oesophagus and include lumps of poorly masticated food (Fig. 2.42), animal bones and other objects. Obstruction by a food bolus is usually confined to the edentulous, or patients with oesophageal strictures. Ingestion of a variety of objects can occur in your children, the psychiatrically disturbed and prisoners (Fig. 2.43). Larger foreign bodies within the

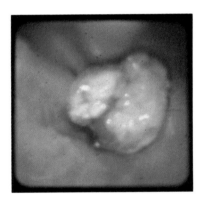

Fig.2.42 Endoscopic view of a bolus of poorly masticated food which has become impacted above a benign oesophageal stricture.

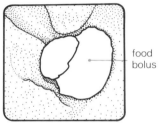

food bolus

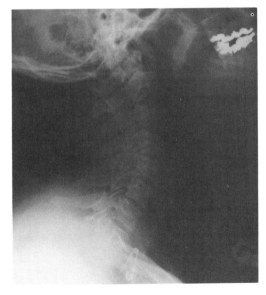

Fig.2.43 Radiograph showing an opened safety-pin impacted in the lower cervical oesophagus of a psychiatrically disturbed patient.

oesophagus tend to stick at the cricopharyngeus, or at the gastro-oesophageal junction. Once objects enter the stomach most will pass through the rest of the gastrointestinal tract uneventfully. Nevertheless, serious complications can occur and these include asphyxiation due to obstruction of the glottis, trachea or major bronchi, oesophageal perforation (Fig. 2.44), or penetration of the aorta or its branches and haemorrhage. For these reasons foreign objects in the upper gastrointestinal tract are frequently removed endoscopically (Fig. 2.45).

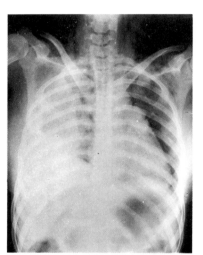

Fig.2.44 Radiograph showing consequences of oesophageal perforation following dilatation of an oesophageal stricture. There is a large right, pleural effusion, mediastinal emphysema and gross surgical emphysema in the neck and upper chest wall.

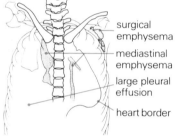

surgical emphysema

mediastinal emphysema

large pleural effusion

heart border

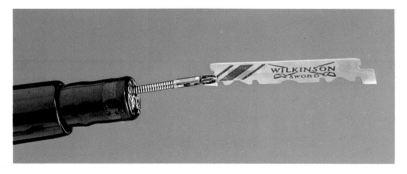

Fig.2.45 Method of removing ingested razor blades endoscopically. The blade is grasped by forceps and the endoscope and blade withdrawn through the oversleeve which protects the pharynx and gastro-oesophageal junction.

Infection

The most important clinical infection of the oesophagus is moniliasis (*Candida*). This may be so mild as to be an incidental finding on endoscopy, or part of a systemic infection severe enough to cause death. Infection with monilia characteristically occurs in individuals with malignant disease, diabetes mellitus, or in patients taking immunosuppressive drugs or antibiotics. Symptoms consist of difficulty and pain on swallowing. At endoscopy *Candida* appears as white adherent patches of varying size which consist of clumps of yeast hyphae superimposed upon a background of hyperaemic and, in severe cases, ulcerated oesophageal mucosa (Fig. 2.46).

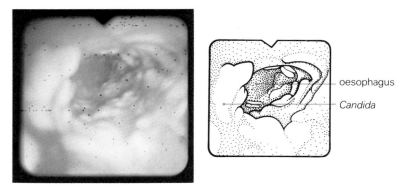

Fig. 2.46 Endoscopic appearance of candidiasis of the oesophagus. The oesophageal mucosa is irregular with a light yellow exudate. There is some redness and a small amount of blood. Courtesy of Dr. F. Silverstein.

The appearance on barium swallow varies from a slight irregularity of the oesophageal wall, which has a fuzzy appearance, to ulceration and nodularity (Fig. 2.47). Exfoliative cytology, direct smears of oesophageal material, and mucosal biopsy may all show yeast forms (Fig. 2.48).

Another important, though less common, infection that may be confused clinically with monilia is herpetic oesophagitis (*Herpes simplex*). This tends to occur in patients on immunosuppressive drugs

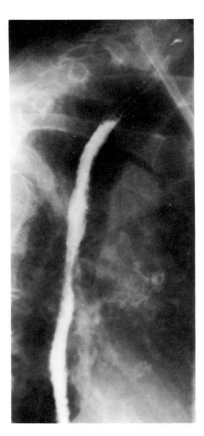
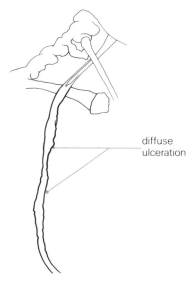

Fig.2.47 Barium swallow showing diffuse candidiasis with diffuse ulceration and narrowing of the oesophagus.

diffuse
ulceration

and in addition to pain and difficulty on swallowing it can lead to bleeding. Confluent or discrete ulceration, or even vesicles may be seen on endoscopy, but the characteristic white patches of moniliasis are absent (Fig. 2.49).

Fig.2.48 A cytological preparation showing candidal hyphae growing outwards from a central fungal ball. Papanicolau stain, x 900. Courtesy of Dr. E. Hudson.

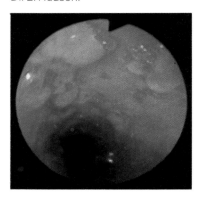

Fig.2.49 Endoscopic view of oesophagitis due to herpes simplex virus showing herpetic vesicles and multiple ulcers.

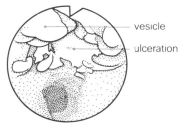

vesicle

ulceration

Oesophageal Varices

Oesophageal varices are submucosal oesophageal veins dilated by increased pressure within the portal venous system. Portal hypertension can be due to chronic liver disease eg. cirrhosis, or thrombosis of the portal vein. Varices are most prominent in the distal oesophagus, although rarely the upper oesophagus may be involved secondary to local obstruction to oesophageal venous drainage within the mediastinum.

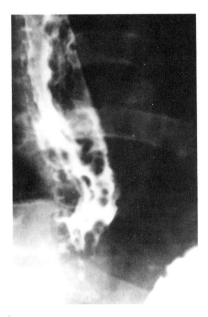

Fig.2.50 Barium swallow in a patient with cirrhosis and portal hypertension showing extensive oesophageal varices.

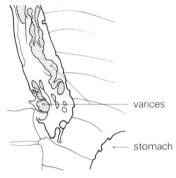

varices

stomach

Fig.2.51 Endoscopic view of large oesophageal varices protruding into the oesophageal lumen.

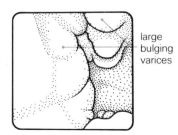

large bulging varices

Varices are an important cause of upper gastro-intestinal bleeding and accurate diagnosis is necessary. A barium swallow following administration of an intravenous anticholinergic drug is useful for demonstrating them (Fig. 2.50), but endoscopy is preferred when there is gastro-intestinal bleeding (Fig. 2.51). This is because it is able to distinguish between variceal and other causes of bleeding, such as a peptic ulcer, which occurs more frequently in patients with cirrhosis.

Other techniques less commonly used for demonstrating varices include the venous phase of splenic arteriography and percutaneous transhepatic portal venography (Fig. 2.52).

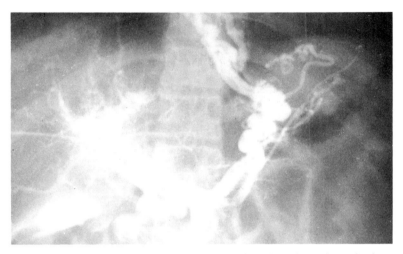

Fig.2.52 Transhepatic portogram in a patient with a thrombosed portal vein following umbillical sepsis in childhood. Note the large collateral gastric vein feeding gastric and oesophageal varices. Courtesy of Dr. R. Dick.

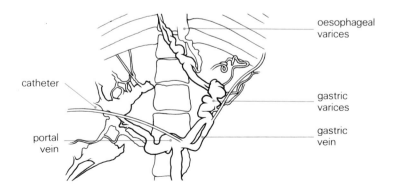

Figure 2.53 shows the macroscopic appearance of ruptured oesophageal varices.

Fig.2.53 Macroscopic appearance of well marked varices in the distal oesophagus with a prominent site of haemorrhage. Courtesy of Dr. D. M. D. Evans.

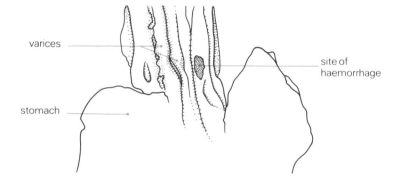

varices

site of
haemorrhage

stomach

The histological appearance of varices is shown in figure 2.54.

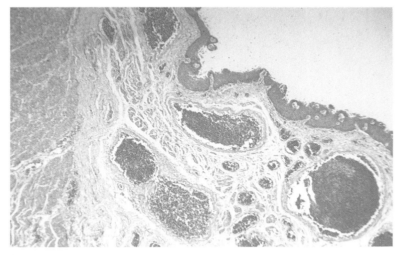

Fig.2.54 Histological appearance of varices. The dilated varices are clearly seen beneath the squamous oesophageal mucosa. H & E stain, x 30.

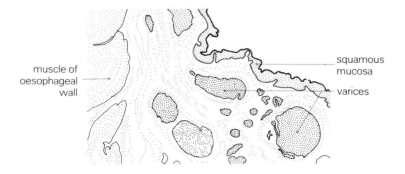

muscle of
oesophageal
wall

squamous
mucosa

varices

3.
Diseases of
the Stomach

Benign Gastric Ulcers

Benign chronic gastric ulcers occur most frequently on the lesser curve of the stomach, although they are also found in the gastric antrum and occasionally on the greater curve. The diagnosis can be established by barium meal examination, when an ulcer crater filled with barium is visible. The differentiation of benign from malignant ulcers is important and for the lesion to be considered benign, radiating mucosal folds

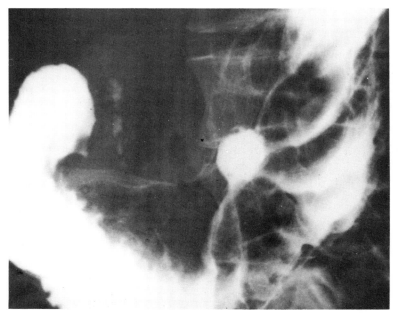

Fig.3.1 Barium meal showing a large, benign, lesser curve gastric ulcer with gastric folds radiating from the edge of the ulcer crater.

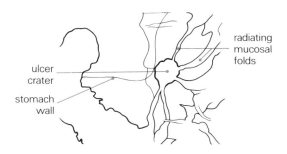

should reach the rim of the ulcer crater (Fig.3.1). However, each patient with a gastric ulcer must be endoscoped to confirm the radiological impression of a benign lesion. An endoscopic view of a chronic lesser curve gastric ulcer shown in figure 3.2 illustrates the benign appearances, namely a flat edge and a clean exudate at the base of the ulcer crater. These characteristics however, should always be confirmed by multiple biopsies and exfoliative brush cytology.

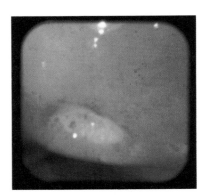

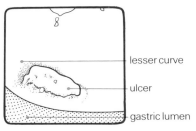

Fig.3.2 Endoscopic view of a chronic lesser curve gastric ulcer.

lesser curve

ulcer

gastric lumen

The macroscopic appearance of a benign gastric ulcer in figure 3.3 (left) shows an ulcer crater on the lesser curve of the stomach and illustrates two points. Firstly, it displays the radiating mucosal folds and secondly it shows the ulcer situated in the body, but close to its junction with the antrum. Benign gastric ulcers usually occur at this site but not in the acid-secreting epithelium. A close-up view of another dissected specimen shows the clean, punched-out appearance of a chronic ulcer with a smooth margin (Fig.3.3, right).

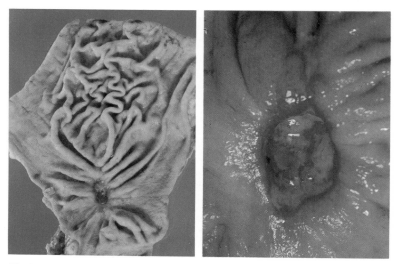

Fig.3.3 A partial gastrectomy specimen showing an oval benign ulcer situated on the lesser curve in the proximal part of the antrum (left), and another specimen showing a chronic ulcer (right).

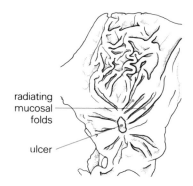

radiating mucosal folds

ulcer

The microscopic features of benign gastric ulcers are illustrated in figures 3.4 and 3.5. Intact gastric mucosa is present at the margins of the ulcer crater (Fig.3.4) and the base of the ulcer consists of granulation and fibrous tissue. In this specimen the fibrosis has not yet involved the muscularis mucosae.

Fig.3.4 The histological appearance of a benign gastric ulcer. Limited fibrosis is present but the muscle coat in the floor of the ulcer is intact. H & E stain, x 12.

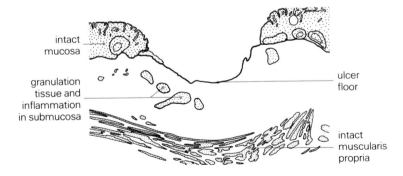

In more chronic ulcers fibrosis can completely replace the gastric muscle, which is then seen only at the margins of the lesion (Fig. 3.5).

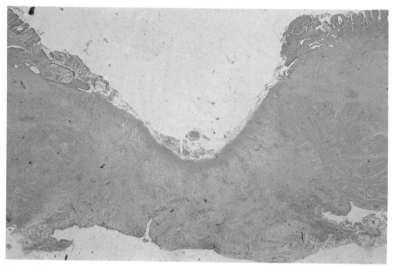

Fig. 3.5 The histological appearance of a chronic, benign, gastric ulcer. In contrast to figure 3.4 there is a complete fibrous replacement of the muscle coat of the stomach wall. Surviving muscle is seen at both edges. H & E stain, x 12.

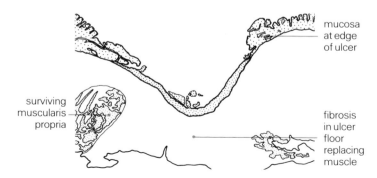

surviving
muscularis
propria

mucosa
at edge
of ulcer

fibrosis
in ulcer
floor
replacing
muscle

Other histological features of a chronic benign gastric ulcer are shown in figure 3.6 where erosion of an artery in the base of the ulcer with subsequent haemorrhage is seen.

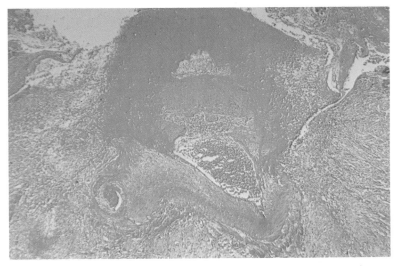

Fig.3.6 Haemorrhage from erosion of an artery in the floor of a benign ulcer. A cap of fibrin and blood is replacing the luminal aspect of the arterial wall. H & E stain, x 30.

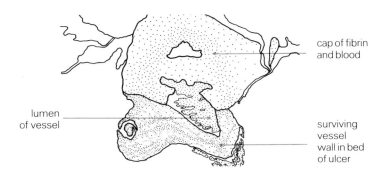

Giant Benign Gastric Ulcers

Giant ulcers are variants of benign gastric ulcers. Apart from their size they carry no special clinical significance. The incidence of malignancy is not increased: the definition of a giant ulcer is simply 'a very large gastric ulcer', and initially it can heal quickly. Figure 3.7 is an example of a large, benign gastric ulcer arising from the lesser curve.

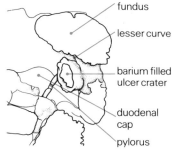

Fig.3.7 Radiograph showing a giant benign gastric ulcer (supine view, double contrast barium meal). The ulcer crater measures 6.5 cm.

- fundus
- lesser curve
- barium filled ulcer crater
- duodenal cap
- pylorus

Juxtapyloric Ulcers

Juxtapyloric ulcers are invariably benign. From the clinical viewpoint they are best grouped with duodenal, rather than with gastric ulcers, as their characteristics resemble the former. They can be demonstrated radiologically, but are best diagnosed endoscopically (Fig. 3.8).

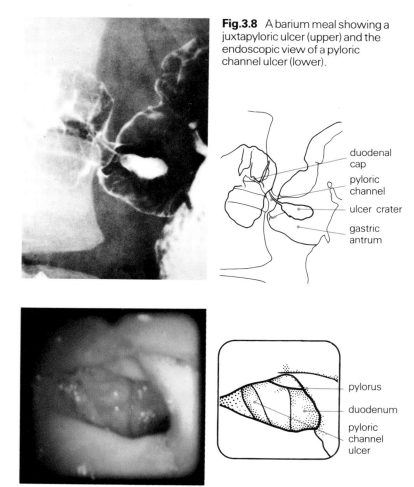

Fig.3.8 A barium meal showing a juxtapyloric ulcer (upper) and the endoscopic view of a pyloric channel ulcer (lower).

duodenal cap

pyloric channel

ulcer crater

gastric antrum

pylorus

duodenum

pyloric channel ulcer

Greater Curve Ulcers

These ulcers can be benign, but are often malignant and should be carefully screened for the presence of carcinoma. A particular variant of this type of ulcer is the 'sump' ulcer that occurs in the most dependent part of the stomach and which may be associated with ingestion of anti-inflammatory drugs. Figure 3.9 demonstrates an endoscopic view of such an ulcer with tablets of a non-steroidal anti-inflammatory drug present within its base.

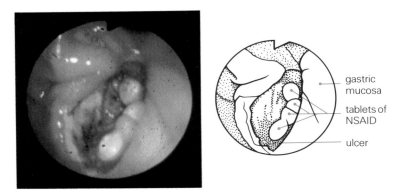

gastric
mucosa

tablets of
NSAID

ulcer

Fig.3.9 Endoscopic view of a greater curve ulcer with tablets of a non-steroidal anti-inflammatory drug (NSAID) lying in its base. Courtesy of Dr. R. Tobias.

Exclusion of Malignancy

Every patient with a gastric ulcer must be endoscoped so that the benign, or malignant nature of the ulcer can be established by targeted, multiple biopsies and by exfoliative cytological brushing. As the distribution of malignant tissue in an ulcer is often focal, the minimun number of biopsies should be five, one from each quadrant of the ulcer rim and one from the base. The chances of detecting a gastric cancer, especially an early gastric cancer, increases as more biopsies are taken. Figure 3.10 shows two biopsies from the same ulcer. One of these is

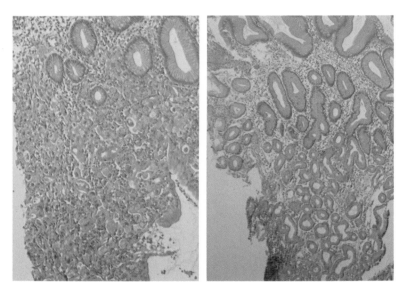

Fig.3.10 Two biopsies from an ulcer, part of an endoscopic series of ten. Only one of the ten (left) showed an infiltrating adenocarcinoma, the others being benign (right). This is an example of the sampling error inherent in endoscopic biopsies. H & E stain, x 75.

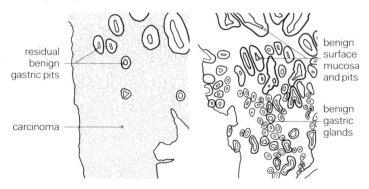

residual benign gastric pits

carcinoma

benign surface mucosa and pits

benign gastric glands

benign, while the other biopsy shows adenocarcinoma. These two biopsies emphasise the need for thorough tissue sampling. Exfoliative cytology is complementary to multiple, targeted biopsy from a gastric ulcer. The cytological appearances of cells from a benign gastric ulcer are contrasted with those from a gastric carcinoma in figure 3.11.

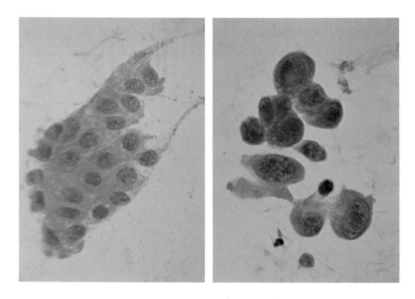

Fig.3.11 Cytological preparations contrasting benign gastric epithelial cells (left) with obviously malignant cells (right). The latter have an increased nuclear cytoplasmic ratio and hyperchromatic nuclei with coarsely-clumped chromatin. Papanicolaou stain, x 5000. Courtesy of Dr. E. A. Hudson.

Complications of Gastric Ulcers

The major complications of gastric ulceration are bleeding and perforation. Figure 3.12 shows a benign lesser curve gastric ulcer with a spurting artery in its base. Perforation of a gastric ulcer may occur into adjacent organs, or into the peritoneal cavity. Perforation of a benign gastric ulcer into the colon forming a gastro-colic fistula is shown radiologically in figure 3.13.

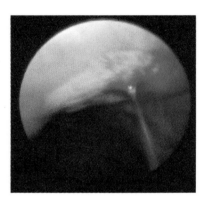

Fig.3.12 Endoscopic view of a benign lesser curve ulcer with a spurting artery in its base. Courtesy of Dr. F. Silverstein.

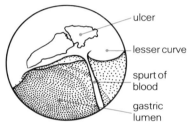

ulcer

lesser curve

spurt of blood

gastric lumen

Fig.3.13 Barium meal showing a gastro-colic fistula. Courtesy of Prof. R. Kottler.

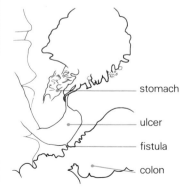

stomach

ulcer

fistula

colon

Hiatus Hernia

A hiatus hernia occurs when part of the stomach protrudes through the diaphragm and lies within the thoracic cavity. The great majority of herniae are of the sliding type, in which a variable portion of the stomach slides up through the diaphragmatic opening, so that the cardio-oesophageal junction lies above the level of the diaphragm. This is often accompanied by weakening of the lower oesophageal sphincter and reflux of gastric contents into the oesophagus. However, reflux may occur in the absence of a hiatus hernia and vice versa. Figure 3.14 illustrates a typical sliding hiatus hernia. This is often associated with

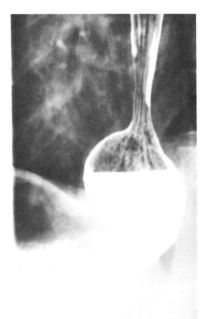

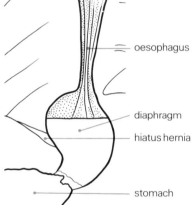

Fig.3.14 Barium meal showing a sliding hiatus hernia.

oesophagus

diaphragm

hiatus hernia

stomach

gastro-oesophageal reflux.

At endoscopy the cardio-oesophageal junction is seen lying above the indentation of the diaphragmatic crura. With the endoscope advanced into the stomach and turned back on itself (the 'J' manoeuvre), a wide, lax gastro-oesophageal junction can be seen around the instrument (Fig.3.15).

A rolling, or para-oesophageal hiatus hernia (Fig.3.16) is much less common. In this type the gastro-oesphageal junction is normally situated below the level of the diaphragm, but a part of the stomach herniates anteriorly through the diaphragm to lie within the thoracic

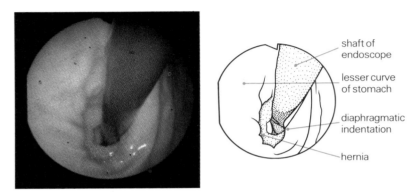

Fig.3.15 Endoscopic view of a hiatus hernia. The retroflexed endoscope is passing through the hernia; the lax mucosal constriction surrounding the shaft of the instrument is due to the diaphragmatic hiatus.

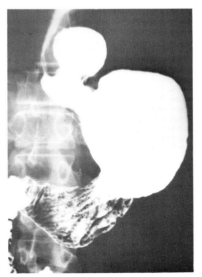

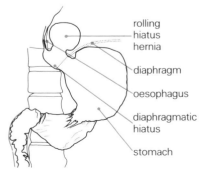

Fig.3.16 Barium meal showing a rolling hiatus hernia.

cavity. Reflux does not necessarily occur, but patients experience a feeling of fullness and discomfort after meals. Complications of this type of hernia are strangulation and infarction. Ulceration of the herniated stomach may occur in either type (Fig.3.17). A small percentage of hiatus herniae are a combination of both the rolling and sliding types.

Gastritis

Gastritis, or inflammation of the gastric mucosa, is usually classified according to morphological criteria.

ACUTE GASTRITIS

Acute gastritis has multiple causes. Different acute mucosal reactions have led to a variety of synonyms including acute erosive gastritis and

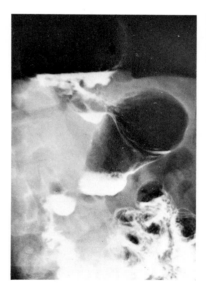

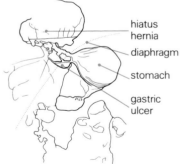

Fig.3.17 Barium meal showing a gastric ulcer above the diaphragmatic hiatus, within a large hiatus hernia.

hiatus hernia

diaphragm

stomach

gastric ulcer

acute haemorrhagic gastritis. Agents that cause acute gastritis include aspirin, alcohol, cytotoxic drugs, gastric irradiation, staphylococcal food poisoning and severe stress, particularly after trauma, or extensive burns. The most important clinical feature of acute gastritis is gastrointestinal haemorrhage, which may be profuse.

Radiology in acute gastritis is only useful if an airbarium double contrast technique is used. This technique demonstrates small shallow ulcers characterised by a central pit of barium surrounded by a lucent halo (Fig.3.18). Endoscopically lesions may appear as multiple haemorrhagic spots and small superficial erosions occurring against the background of hyperaemia (Fig.3.19). These may be widespread thoughout the stomach (Fig.3.20).

The lesions of acute gastritis are seldom biopsied but may show a

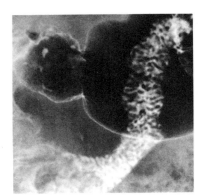

Fig.3.18 Barium meal showing erosions.

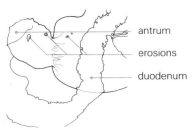

antrum

erosions

duodenum

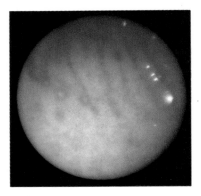

Fig.3.19 Endoscopic view of gastric erosions in association with linear haemorrhages.

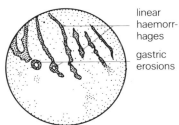

linear
haemorr-
hages

gastric
erosions

spectrum of histological changes from superficial haemorrhage to complete mucosal necrosis, depending on the aetiology. The commonest picture corresponding to an erosion, is of an acute inflammatory cell infiltrate restricted to the superficial part of the gastric mucosa and accompanied by focal loss of the surface epithelium (Fig.3.21).

CHRONIC GASTRITIS

Chronic gastritis can be divided into two broad categories. The first (type A) involves the body of the stomach, usually spares the antrum

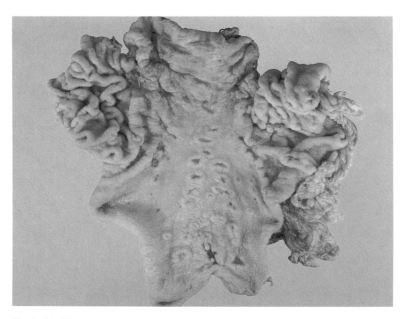

Fig.3.20 The macroscopic appearance of multiple small gastric erosions distributed along the length of the lesser curve, each with an elevated margin.

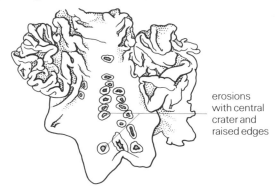

erosions with central crater and raised edges

and is associated with parietal cell antibodies, reduced acid and intrinsic factor secretion and hence vitamin B_{12} malabsorption. Patients with pernicious anaemia fall within this category and there is an association between type A gastritis and other autoimmune disorders, eg. Hashimoto's and Addison's disease.

In the second pattern (type B), parietal cell antibodies are absent. Acid secretion may be moderately reduced, but impairment of B_{12} absorption is rare. The changes are maximal in the antrum but often focal and extend for a variable distance along the lesser curve. Endoscopically, severe atrophic gastritis and gastric atrophy is

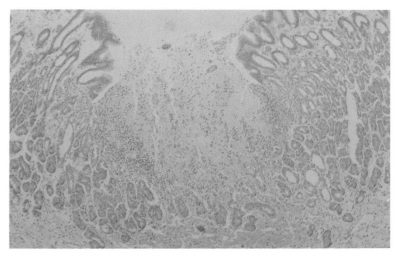

Fig.3.21 Histological appearance of an acute gastric erosion. There is necrosis of the superficial two thirds of the mucosa. A cuff of inflammatory cells separates this area from the surviving mucosa. H & E stain, x 75.

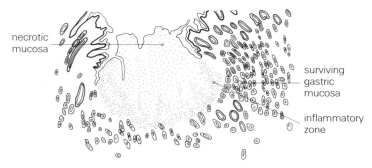

necrotic mucosa

surviving gastric mucosa

inflammatory zone

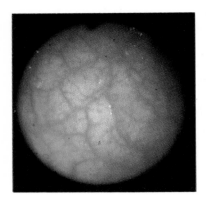

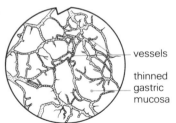

Fig.3.22 Endoscopic view in chronic gastritis.

vessels

thinned gastric mucosa

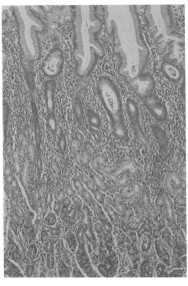

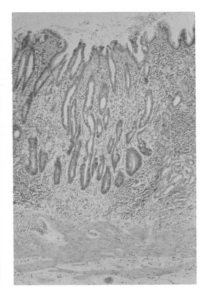

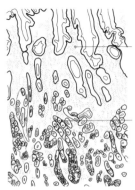

inflamed superficial mucosa

acid secreting gastric mucosa

metaplastic epithelium with goblet cells

surviving antral glands

inflammation

recognised by a thinned mucosa with prominent submucosal vessels (Fig.3.22). Lesser degrees of atrophic gastritis can, however, only be diagnosed by biopsy.

The histological changes in chronic gastritis consist of mucosal inflammation with progressive glandular atrophy and concurrent intestinal metaplasia (Fig.3.23). In its most severe form this is known as gastric atrophy and is a common pattern in pernicious anaemia. Within a population most of the elderly will have some degree of antral pattern gastritis which is slowly progressive. It is said that 10% of patients with established chronic atrophic gastritis unassociated with pernicious anaemia may develop a gastric carcinoma.

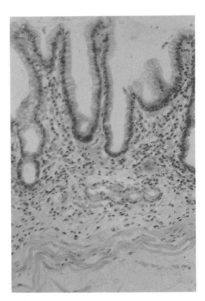

Fig.3.23 A histological series showing the progession of chronic gastritis. On the left the inflammatory infiltrate is mainly restricted to the gastric pits; the gastric glands are not yet involved by the inflammatory process. In the middle section the infiltrate is extending down through the glands which are now reduced in number. On the right atrophic gastritis is established. The inflammation is muted and there is little specialised glandular tissue remaining: H & E stain, x 50.

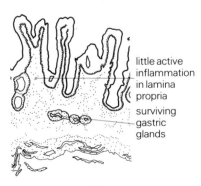

little active inflammation in lamina propria

surviving gastric glands

This is a disorder of unknown aetiology in which there is diffuse infiltration of the distal stomach with eosinophils; peripheral eosinophilia is usually present. A similar process may affect the whole intestinal tract and the cellular infiltrate may extend from mucosa to serosa. Mucosal involvement gives rise to thickened antral folds that may cause pyloric obstruction, bleeding or loss of plasma protein. Serosal involvement can cause eosinophilic ascites. Histologically the changes are best seen in the antrum. There is submucosal oedema and a variable infiltrate of eosinophils throughout the stomach wall (Fig. 3.24, left). Occasional giant cells may be present.

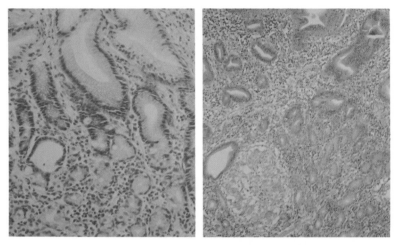

Fig.3.24 Eosinophilic gastritis showing red-staining eosinophils throughout the mucosa (left, carbol chromotrope stain, x 320). Granulomatous gastritis with a well-formed granuloma and adjacent intestinal metaplasia (right, H & E stain, x 50).

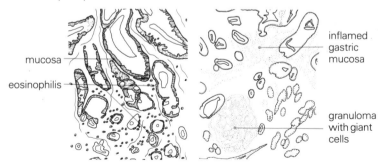

GRANULOMATOUS GASTRITIS

Isolated granulomatous gastritis is a diagnosis of exclusion since clinically, radiologically and histologically it resembles tuberculosis, sarcoidosis, or Crohn's desease of the stomach, but without the systemic features. Macroscopically the appearances include narrowing of the pyloric canal, ulceration, and infiltration and thickening of the gastric mucosa resembling 'linitis plastica'. Histologically, the diagnosis depends on the identification of giant cell granulomas within the mucosa (Fig. 3.24, right). An associated gastritis may, or may not be present.

GIANT HYPERTROPHIC GASTRITIS

Giant hypertrophic gastritis, or Menetrier's disease is an uncommon condition in which there is generalised, or localised enlargement of the gastric folds normally affecting the body of the stomach and which radiologically suggests gastric polyposis, carcinoma or giant rugal hypertrophy. The giant folds are easily seen endoscopically and they may have a nodular or polypoid appearance (Fig. 3.25).

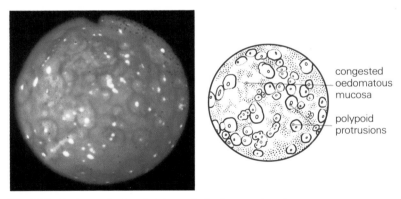

congested oedomatous mucosa

polypoid protrusions

Fig.3.25 Endoscopic view in Menetrier's disease showing numerous polypoid protrusions and congested oedematous gastric mucosa.

The surface is frequently congested, eroded (Fig.3.26, left) or ulcerated leading to the protein loss and hypoproteinaemia which is a characteristic of the condition. The biopsy must be deep to be helpful and shows elongation and dilatation of the gastric pits (Fig.3.26, right). There is some replacement of the acid-secreting glands by simple mucus glands and many of these become cystic. A mild gastritis may also be present.

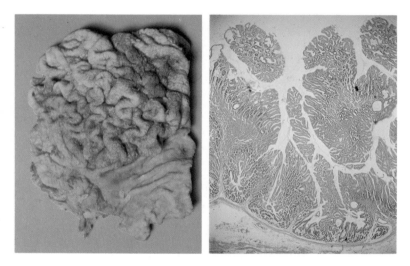

Fig.3.26 The stomach in Menetrier's disease with grossly enlarged mucosal folds but sparing the antrum (left). The microscopy of Menetrier's disease (right, H & E stain, x 8) illustrates the great increase in depth and complexity of the gastric pits in the folds of gastric mucosa.

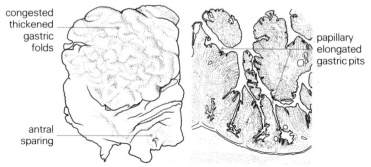

congested thickened gastric folds

antral sparing

papillary elongated gastric pits

Carcinoma

Gastric carcinoma is one of the commonest gastro-intestinal malignancies, although its occurrence appears to be decreasing the Western world. Nevertheless, certain countries such a Chile and Japan continue to have an unenviably high incidence of the disease. Patients usually present late, although early gastric cancer, which carries a good prognosis, is being increasingly recognised. Gastric carcinomas occur most commonly in the antrum and on the lesser curve of the stomach and may have a variety of macroscopic appearances which include overtly neoplastic ulcers with rolled edges (Fig.3.27), fungating

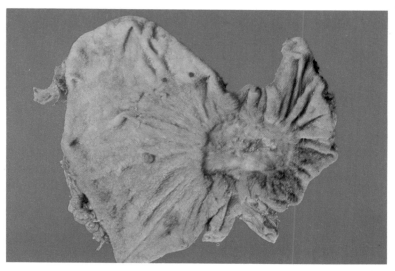

Fig.3.27 A partial gastrectomy specimen showing a large, lesser curve malignant ulcer with raised rolled margins.

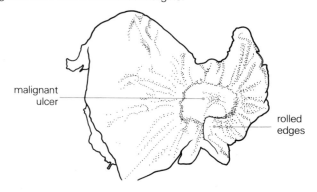

tumours, nodular tumours (Figs.3.28-3.30) and even some apparently benign-looking ulcers. A less common variety of gastric carcinoma is

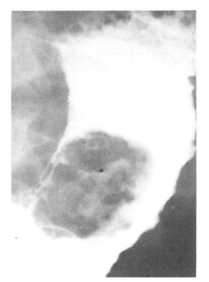

Fig.3.28 Barium meal showing a large polypoid carcinoma in the body of the stomach causing a filling defect.

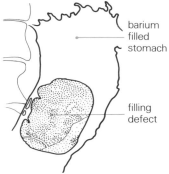

barium
filled
stomach

filling
defect

Fig.3.29 Endoscopic view of a fungoid carcinoma.

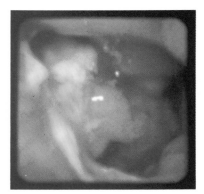

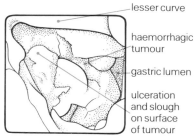

lesser curve

haemorrhagic
tumour

gastric lumen

ulceration
and slough
on surface
of tumour

the infiltrating type known as 'linitis plastica', in which the malignant growth spreads widely throughout all layers of the stomach wall

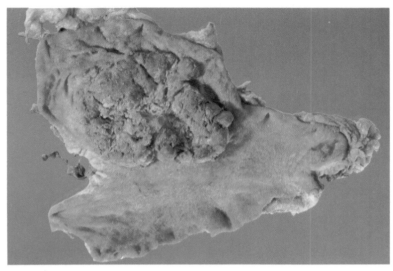

Fig.3.30 A fungating carcinoma occupying the lesser curve of the stomach.

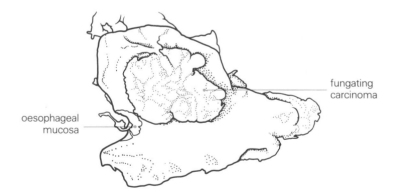

fungating carcinoma

oesophageal mucosa

(Figs. 3.31 & 3.32). In this type of carcinoma ulceration of the mucosa may be minimal, or absent. Endoscopic biopsy and exfoliative cytology are mandatory in any potentially neoplastic lesion of the stomach.

The most common microscopic classification of gastric cancer is into

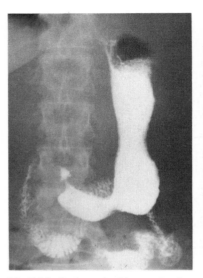

Fig. 3.31 Barium meal (erect view) showing the typical appearance of an extensive 'linitis plastica' involving the entire stomach. The stomach was fixed and narrowed. No peristalsis was seen. The mucosal edge is only slightly irregular. Barium flowed out of the stomach quickly.

Fig. 3.32 A partial gastrectomy from a case of 'linitis plastica' showing the greatly thickened wall and the diffuse nature of the malignancy – a nodular mucosal surface with no single discrete tumour focus.

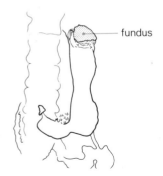

fundus

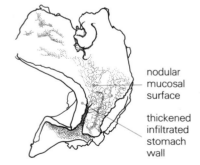

nodular mucosal surface

thickened infiltrated stomach wall

two types, namely the intestinal and the diffuse. In the intestinal form the glandular pattern is obvious (Fig. 3.33) and the tumour forms a well-defined expanding mass. It is the commonest variety in geographical areas with a high incidence.

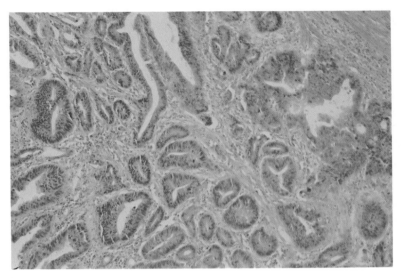

Fig.3.33 Histological appearance of an intestinal type carcinoma showing well-formed malignant glandular elements. H & E stain, x 75.

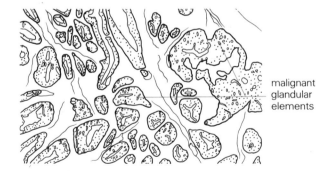

malignant glandular elements

The diffuse pattern has ill-defined infiltrative edges and the tumour cells are solitary or are arranged in small clusters (Fig.3.34). Gland formation is rare. This pattern is seen in areas with a low incidence of gastric cancer and within a younger population than the intestinal variety.

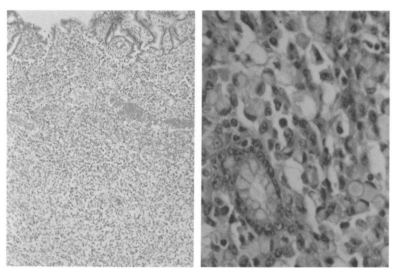

Fig.3.34 A diffuse pattern gastric carcinoma. No tubular pattern is shown in the low power view (left, H & E stain, x 50). In the high power view (right, H & E stain, x 320) the discrete nature of the mucin-laden tumour cells (signet ring cells) is apparent in contrast to the surviving pyloric gland.

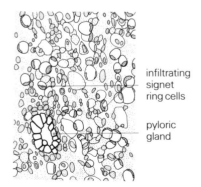

infiltrating signet ring cells

pyloric gland

Early gastric carcinoma is defined as carcinoma confined to the mucosa or submucosa, even though lymph node metastases can be present at the time of diagnosis. It is infrequently recognised in the West, but mass screening programmes in Japan have shown that such cancers may account for 30% of gastric carcinomas in that country. Radiologically, early gastric cancer can appear as a small, irregular elevated area or ulcer (Fig.3.35) and similar appearances may be seen

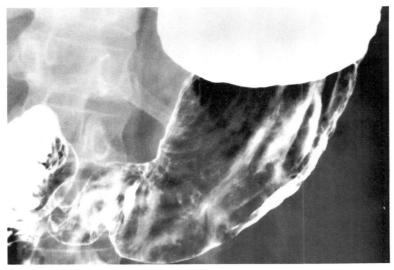

Fig.3.35 Barium meal showing early gastric cancer. The edge of the infiltrated area is outlined by barium. There is angular cut off of the gastric folds at this edge. The lesser curve is deformed. The abnormal folds are an important radiological sign of early gastric cancer. Courtesy of Dr. G. J. de Lacey.

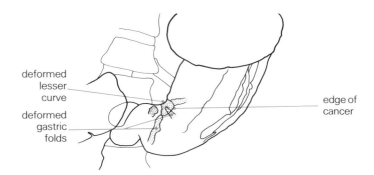

at endoscopy (Fig.3.36). The accepted classification is based on the macroscopic appearances at endoscopy (Fig.3.37).

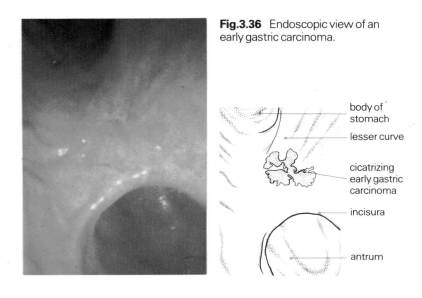

Fig.3.36 Endoscopic view of an early gastric carcinoma.

body of stomach

lesser curve

cicatrizing early gastric carcinoma

incisura

antrum

Fig.3.37 The macroscopic classification of early gastric carcinoma based on endoscopic appearances.

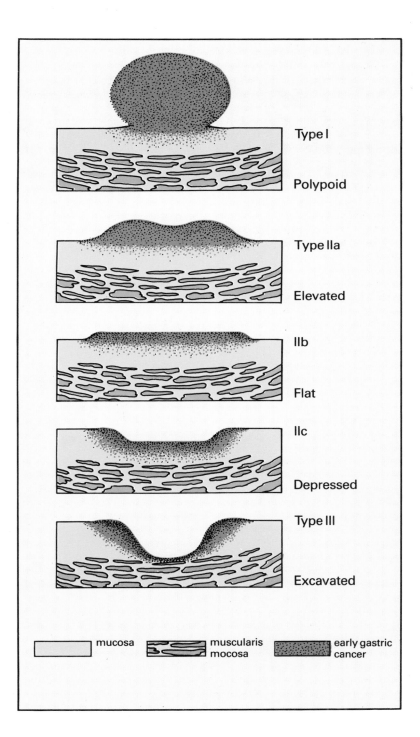

Type I

Polypoid

Type IIa

Elevated

IIb

Flat

IIc

Depressed

Type III

Excavated

mucosa   muscularis mocosa   early gastric cancer

Multiple biopsies and exfoliative cytology are always necessary to confirm the diagnosis. Some of the various types of early gastric carcinoma are illustrated in the resected specimens shown in figure 3.38. The histological patterns of early gastric cancer are similar to

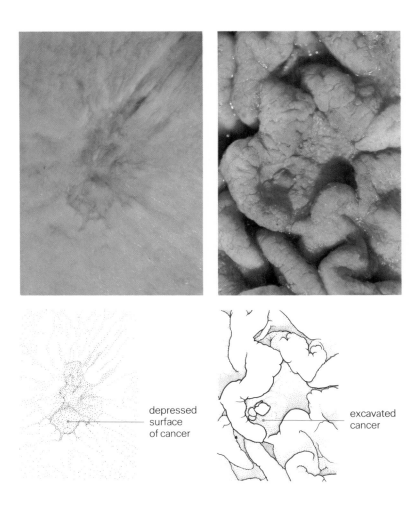

depressed surface of cancer

excavated cancer

Fig.3.38 Some of the macroscopic varieties of early gastric cancer: the depressed type, type IIc (left); the excavated type, type III (middle); the protruding type, type I (right).

polypoid
cancer

their advanced counterparts. Well differentiated tumour with obvious glandular formation is more common in the protruberant types and poorly differentiated tumour with signet-ring cell carcinoma is more common in the flat and excavated lesion (Fig. 3.39).

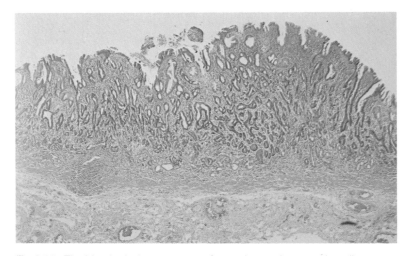

Fig.3.39 The histological appearance of an early gastric cancer invading the mucosa but not extending through the muscularis (intestinal type). H & E stain, x 30.

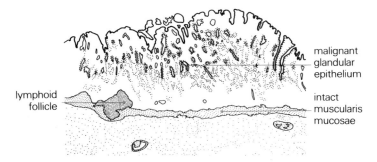

lymphoid follicle

malignant glandular epithelium

intact muscularis mucosae

Certain conditions are associated with an increased risk of developing gastric carcinoma. These include pernicious anaemia, adenomatous polyps, intestinal metaplasia (Fig.3.40) and previous gastric surgery.

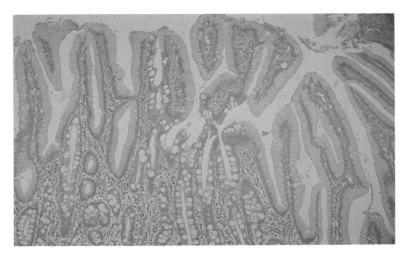

Fig.3.40 Intestinal metaplasia. The uniform columnar cells of the normal gastric epithelium clearly contrast with the apparently vacuolated goblet cells of the metaplastic epithelium. H & E stain, x 75.

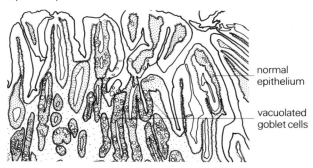

normal epithelium

vacuolated goblet cells

Lymphoma
The stomach may be involved by lymphoma, either as an isolated lesion or as part of a disseminated process. Several differing gross appearances can occur, including ulcerated and polypoid lesions, diffuse infiltration and rugal hypertrophy. The radiological appearances reflect the various types and figure 3.41 demonstrates diffuse infiltration of the

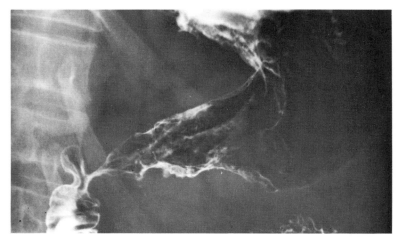

Fig.3.41 Barium meal showing a large, irregular, annular mass in the antrum and distal body of the stomach extending into the duodenum, which was a lymphoma. The wall thickening around the tumour mass is just visible.

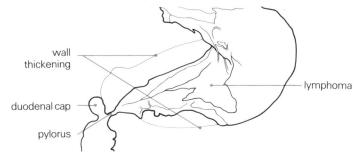

stomach and duodenal wall by a gastric lymphoma. Endoscopically they mimic carcinomas with ulcerated lesions often having proliferative rolled edges (Fig.3.42) and a large biopsy, which includes submucosa, may be needed for histological proof. A surgical specimen is shown in figure 3.43.

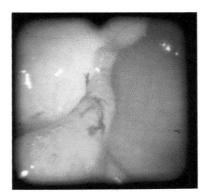

Fig.3.42 Endoscopic view of a gastric lymphoma.

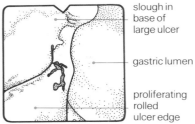

slough in base of large ulcer

gastric lumen

proliferating rolled ulcer edge

Microscopically, the commonest pattern is a lymphosarcoma comprising diffuse sheets of maturing lymphocytes (Fig.3.44). The infiltrate is often confined to the mucosa and submucosa for a prolonged period before full thickness involvement of the stomach wall occurs. All cytological patterns of lymphoma may occur in the stomach, including

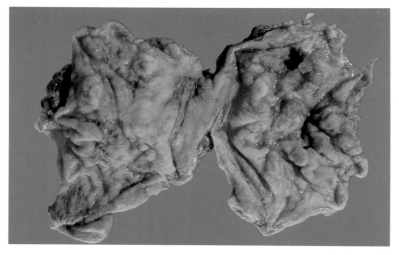

Fig.3.43 A partial gastrectomy showing the nodular mucosa associated with a widespread gastric lymphoma.

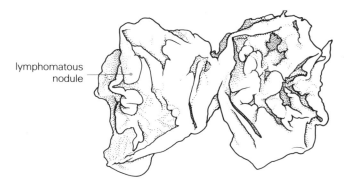

lymphomatous nodule

Hodgkin's disease, and histiocytic and plasmacytic lymphomas. A rare form of benign follicular lymphoid hyperplasia (pseudolymphoma) restricted to the mucosa also occurs, and must be distinguished from a malignant lymphoma.

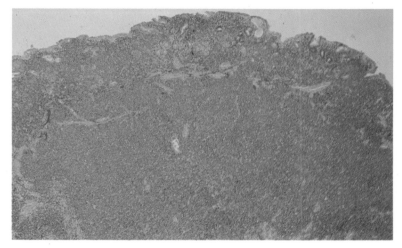

Fig.3.44 Diffuse lymphosarcomatous infiltration obliterating the mucosa and submucosa. A few glands are surviving. H & E stain, x 30.

Leiomyoma
Leiomyomas are rare, but are the most common benign tumours of the stomach. They arise from the gastric smooth muscle and are frequently

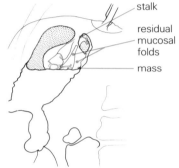

Fig.3.45 An oblique view of the fundus showing a large polypoid mass with a smooth surface and stretched, residual, mucosal folds extending over its surface. This was due to an intramural leiomyoma.

stalk

residual mucosal folds

mass

asymptomatic. Radiologically they appear as smooth filling defects and may be pedunculated (Fig.3.45). Classically, an ulcerated polypoid and obviously submucosal tumour is present (Fig.3.46), the common

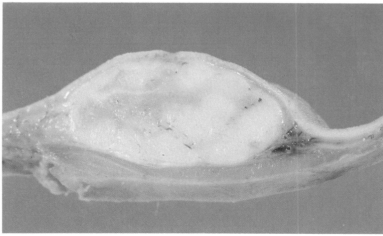

Fig.3.46 An ulcerated leiomyoma arising from the antrum (upper). The cut surface of these tumours emphasises their submucosal character (lower).

occurrence of haemorrhage being due to the ulceration (Fig.3.47). Less commonly pyloric obstruction may occur. Histology of a typical tumour shows interlacing bundles and whorls of smooth muscle cells (Fig.3.48). The problem in smooth muscle tumours is to predict their behaviour. Although size and mitotic activity are valuable indicators, the only reliable evidence of malignancy is the presence of metastases. An 'epithelioid' variety of smooth muscle tumour is described (leiomyoblastoma) that behaves in a similar fashion.

Other, non-epithelial tumours, such as lipomas and neural sheath tumours, also occur within the stomach.

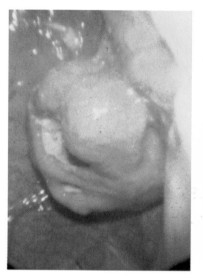

Fig.3.47 Endoscopic view of a leiomyoma: the polypoid lesion is protruding into the gastric lumen.

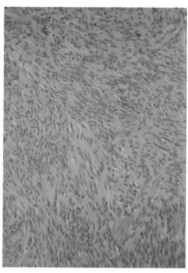

Fig.3.48 Histological appearance of a typical leiomyoma showing the interlacing bundles of smooth muscle. H & E stain, x 120.

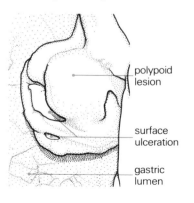

polypoid lesion

surface ulceration

gastric lumen

Diverticula

Gastric diverticula are uncommon chance radiological findings. The majority are congenital and occur high on the posterior wall of the stomach just below the gastro-oesophageal junction (Fig. 3.49, upper). A small percentage are pre-pyloric and usually associated with previous peptic ulceration. Endoscopically they appear as a small round opening with sharp margins, which alter with peristalsis (Fig. 3.49, lower). Their clinical significance is questionable, but occasionally dyspepsia, or symptoms of post-prandial vomiting and nausea lead to resection.

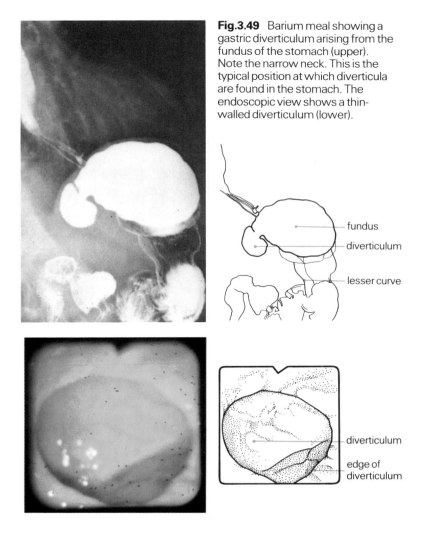

Fig.3.49 Barium meal showing a gastric diverticulum arising from the fundus of the stomach (upper). Note the narrow neck. This is the typical position at which diverticula are found in the stomach. The endoscopic view shows a thin-walled diverticulum (lower).

fundus

diverticulum

lesser curve

diverticulum

edge of diverticulum

Polyps

Gastric polyps are hamartomatous, regenerative/hyperplastic, or true neoplasms (adenomas). It is only the latter group that have any important malignant potential. They may also be associated with pernicious anaemia. Polyps appear on radiographs as multiple or single,

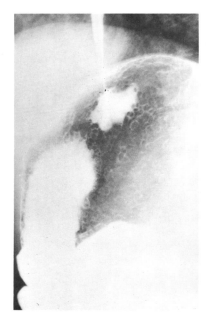

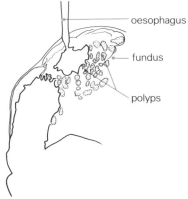

Fig.3.50 Barium meal showing numerous filling defects due to small sessile hamartomatous polyps.

oesophagus

fundus

polyps

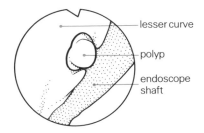

Fig.3.51 Endoscopic view of an adenomatous polyp.

lesser curve

polyp

endoscope shaft

round translucent filling defects within the stomach (Fig. 3.50). Sessile polyps larger than two centimetres in diameter are more likely to be malignant. At endoscopy adenomatous polyps look more hyperaemic than the surrounding mucosa (Fig. 3.51). The regenerative or hyperplastic polyp is the commonest in clinical practice (Fig. 3.52).

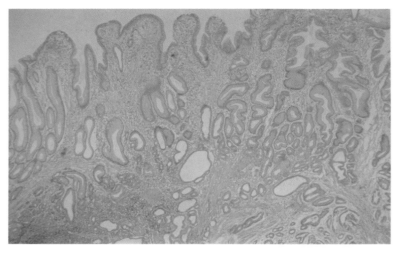

Fig.3.52 Histological appearance of a hyperplastic polyp showing the deranged mucosal architecture (irregular, elongated, cystic gastric pits) but without dysplastic changes. H & E stain, x 30.

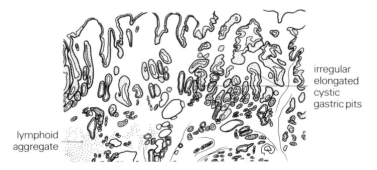

irregular
elongated
cystic
gastric pits

lymphoid
aggregate

Gastric Surgery

Gastric surgery for benign peptic ulcer disease usually consists of acid-reducing operation combined with a drainage procedure. The drainage procedure is necessary as gastric motility is decreased by vagotomy. Thus truncal vagotomy is combined with pyloroplasty, gastro-enterostomy or antrectomy.

Highly selective vagotomy which preserves the innervation of the antrum (nerves of Laterjet) does not require an additional drainage

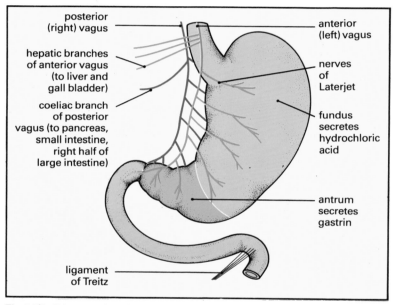

Fig.3.53 Diagram showing the normal anatomy and physiology of the stomach. Courtesy of Prof. M. Hobsley.

procedure, because the function of the antral pump, and therefore gastric emptying is not disturbed.

Less commonly a Polya partical gastrectomy for recurrent duodenal ulceration or pyloric canal obstruction, a Bilroth I partial gastrectomy for a gastric ulcer or a total gastrectomy for patients with a gastric carcinoma or the Zollinger-Ellison syndrome in whom medical treatment has failed, is performed. These types of gastric operations and the normal anatomy and physiology of the stomach are represented diagrammatically in figures 3.53-3.55.

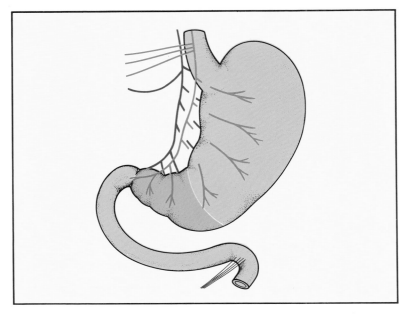

Fig.3.54 The highly selective vagotomy. This procedure denervates the fundus, not the antrum or gastric structures. Courtesy of Prof. M. Hobsley.

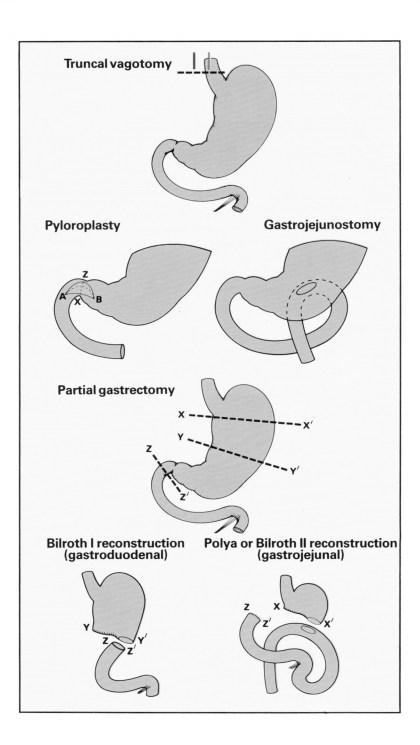

Truncal vagotomy

Pyloroplasty

Gastrojejunostomy

Partial gastrectomy

Bilroth I reconstruction
(gastroduodenal)

Polya or Bilroth II reconstruction
(gastrojejunal)

The altered anatomy following surgery is readily seen at endoscopy and figure 3.56 shows the appearance of the afferent and efferent loops following a Polya gastrectomy.

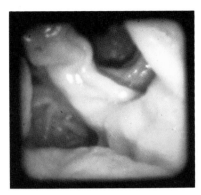

Fig.3.56 Endoscopic view of the afferent and efferent loops following a Polya gastrectomy.

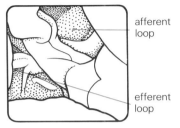

afferent loop

efferent loop

Fig.3.55 Truncal vagotomy, pyloroplasty, gastrojejunostomy and partial gastrectomy. The truncal vagotomy denervates the whole stomach (fundus plus antrum) as well as the liver, gallbladder, pancreas, small intestine and right half of the colon. In pyloroplasty, an incision is made from A to B across the pylorus which is then sutured from X to Z thus widening the lumen of the pyloric channel. Alternatively in gastrojejunostomy, a loop of jejunum is sutured to the posterior/inferior wall of the stomach to provide adequate drainage. In partial gastrectomy two thirds of the stomach is resected between XX' and ZZ', or a more localised resection ('antrectomy') may be performed, between YY' and ZZ'. Courtesy of Prof. M. Hobsley.

Other features which may be seen endoscopically following gastric surgery include ulceration of the stoma, in particular following a Polya gastrectomy (Fig.3.57) or a retained suture (Fig.3.58). These retained sutures are usually innocent, although occasionally they may act as a nidus for ulceration. Another feature commonly seen at endoscopy after gastric surgery is the presence of gastritis due to the reflux of alkaline bile and pancreatic juice. The histological appearances of reflux gastritis are non-specific.

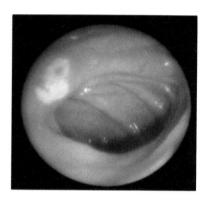

Fig.3.57 Endoscopic view showing ulceration of the stoma.

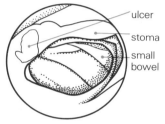

Fig.3.58 Endoscopic view of a retained suture.

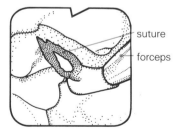

Foreign Bodies and Bezoars

A large variety of foreign bodies may be swallowed. The majority eventually pass spontaneously per rectum although sharp or impacted objects may occasionally need endoscopic removal. Surgery is rarely required. Objects swallowed by an emotionally disturbed young girl are shown on the plain abdominal radiograph in figure 3.59. All of these objects including the needles were passed without mishap.

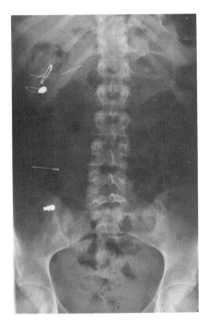

Fig.3.59 Radiograph showing various objects swallowed by an emotionally disturbed young girl. Courtesy of Dr. H. Shawdon.

Bezoars are concretions of foreign material which build up in the stomach and are usually composed either of hair which has been chewed (trichobezoar, Fig.3.60), or of vegetable and plant material (phytobezoar), due to stasis after gastric surgery. Bezoars can give rise to anorexia and vomiting, ulceration, perforation, or obstruction. They can be removed endoscopically or surgically.

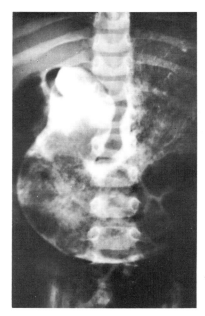

Fig.3.60 Barium meal showing a trichobezoar as a large, irregular, filling defect within the lumen and extending from the fundus to the antrum. This five year old had swallowed cotton wool and her own hair.

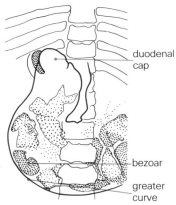

duodenal cap

bezoar

greater curve

4.
Normal Duodenum and Duodenal Disease

Normal Anatomy

The duodenum is the most proximal and fixed part of the small intestine, and joins the stomach to the jejunum. It is approximately 20-30cm in length and it is arbitrarily divided into four parts corresponding to the duodenal bulb, and the descending, horizontal and ascending portions (Fig. 4.1). A barium meal shows the duodenal bulb to be triangular (Fig. 4.2)

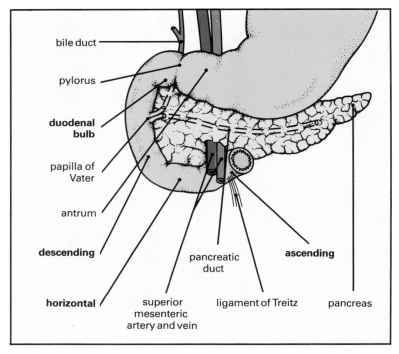

Fig.4.1 Diagram showing the anatomical relationships of the duodenum.

with shallow longitudinal folds that become obliterated when the cap is distended (Fig.4.3). The second part of the duodenum descends retroperitioneally on the right of the midline at the level of the first and second lumbar vertebrae. It lies close to the head of the pancreas and the papilla of Vater (duodenal ampulla) opens on its medial wall at approximately the mid-point (Fig.4.1).

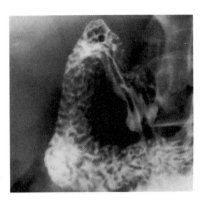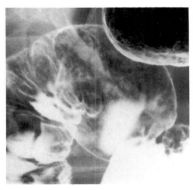

Fig.4.2 Barium meal: compression view of the duodenal cap showing longitudinal folds.

Fig.4.3 Double contrast view of the duodenal cap with the cap distended and the folds effaced. Note the transverse fold pattern of the valvulae conniventes that starts at the junction of the first and second parts of the loop.

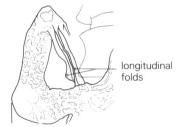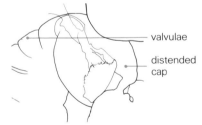

longitudinal folds

valvulae

distended cap

The papilla can be more easily recognised endoscopically by its relationship to the longitudinal fold (Fig. 4.4). The pancreatic duct and the common bile duct enter the duodenum at the papilla (Fig. 4.5). The detailed anatomy of the bile and pancreatic ducts is described elsewhere. The mucosal appearance of the second part of the duodenum is quite different from the smooth lining of the duodenal bulb, for it has the circular folds characteristic of the small intestine, the valvulae conniventes (Fig. 4.6). The third part of the duodenum is also

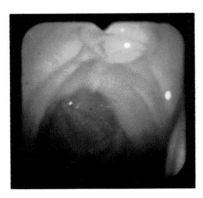

Fig. 4.4 Endoscopic view of the papilla of Vater in relationship to the longitudinal fold.

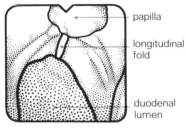

papilla

longitudinal fold

duodenal lumen

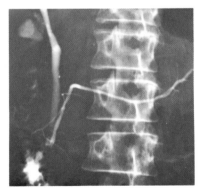

Fig. 4.5 Normal ERCP showing the pancreatic, duct of Santorini and the common bile duct entering at the papilla.

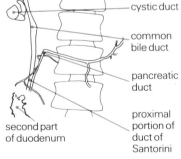

cystic duct

common bile duct

pancreatic duct

proximal portion of duct of Santorini

second part of duodenum

retroperitoneal, crosses the midline at the level of the third lumbar vertebrum and continues close to the head of the pancreas. This part of the duodenum is crossed anteriorly by the superior mesenteric artery and vein (Fig.4.1). The fourth part of the duodenum ascends obliquely before turning abruptly downwards and anteriorly, where its junction with the jejunum is anchored by a fibromuscular structure, the ligament of Treitz. Lying above the fourth part of the duodenum is the body of the pancreas.

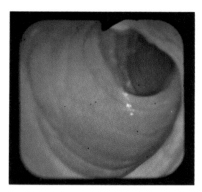

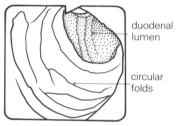

Fig.4.6 Endoscopic view of the second part of the duodenum.

duodenal lumen

circular folds

The normal histology of the duodenum comprises mucosa, muscularis mucosae, submucosa and the circular and longitudinal muscle coat (Fig. 4.7). In the submucosa, unique to the duodenum are Brunner's glands. They secrete mucus and open into the crypts of Lieberkühn at the base of the villi. The muscularis mucosae is often broken up around the glandular elements. Brunner's glands are most numerous in the first part of the duodenum, decreasing distally. The mucosa, in common with the rest of the small bowel, has tall villi between which are the crypts of Lieberkühn that dip down to the muscularis mucosae. The surface epithelium of the villi and crypts is a mixture of absorptive cells and goblet cells. The former have prominent microvilli on their luminal border. There is a gradual maturation of cells from the crypt base to the tip of the villus. Paneth cells and cells of the APUD system are also to be found within the crypts. In general the duodenal villi are slightly broader than those in the jejunum.

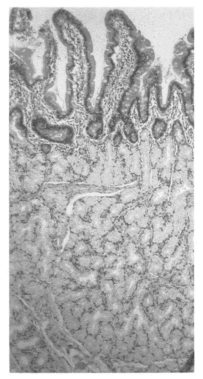

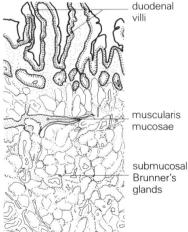

Fig. 4.7 Histological appearance of normal duodenal mucosa. H & E stain, x 100.

duodenal villi

muscularis mucosae

submucosal Brunner's glands

Duodenal Ulcer

Although duodenal ulceration is the commonest non-infective disorder of the upper gastrointestinal tract its aetiology remains completely unknown. Nevertheless, epidemiological and gastric acid secretory studies may identify individuals more likely to develop a duodenal ulcer. Males are more commonly affected than females in a ratio of 3.5:1 and in England 10% of males will have, or have had, a duodenal ulcer at some time of their lives. There is a familial disposition with a higher incidence of the disease in patients of blood group O, those unable to secrete AB substances into saliva or gastric juice, and in individuals with high serum, or mucosal levels of pepsinogen I.

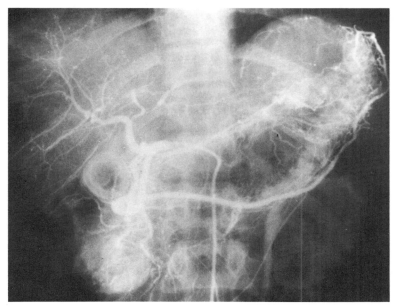

Fig.4.8 Arteriogram showing a gastrinoma.

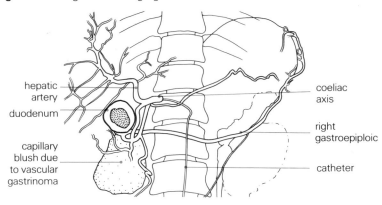

131

Other factors apparently important in the aetiology of duodenal ulceration include smoking, drugs and concomitant disease, for example, chronic obstructive airway disease and polycythaemia rubra vera. Duodenal ulcers do not occur in the absence of acid and most, although not all, patients with duodenal ulceration secrete more gastric acid in response to a histamine, or pentagastrin stimulus. In addition they have higher basal and nocturnal amounts of acid. Patients with a

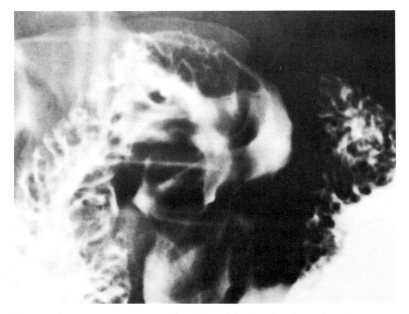

Fig.4.9 Barium meal: compression view of the duodenal cap showing a large central ulcer niche with radiating folds.

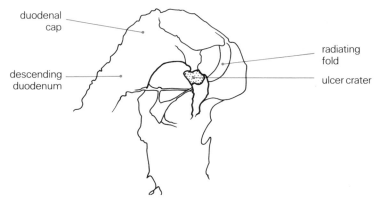

duodenal
cap

radiating
fold

descending
duodenum

ulcer crater

gastrin-producing adenoma of the pancreas (Fig. 4.8), the Zollinger-Ellison syndrome, have gross acid hypersecretion and nearly always have intractable duodenal ulcers. Over 90% of all duodenal ulcers are in the duodenal bulb and the diagnosis is confirmed either by barium meal when a barium-filled niche is visible (Fig. 4.9), or by endoscopy (Fig. 4.10). Ulcers occur most commonly on the anterior wall of the bulb and to a lesser extent the posterior or superior walls (Fig. 4.11).

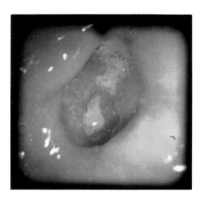

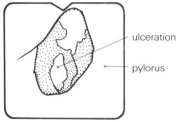

Fig. 4.10 Endoscopic view showing ulceration and surrounding duct.

ulceration

pylorus

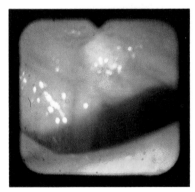

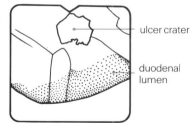

Fig. 4.11 Endoscopic view of a duodenal ulcer on the superior wall of the bulb.

ulcer crater

duodenal lumen

Occasionally anterior and posterior ulcers occur simultaneously ('kissing ulcers') (Fig. 4.12). Unlike gastric ulcers, true duodenal ulcers are never malignant. It is therefore unnecessary to perform endoscopy and biopsy if the diagnosis has been established radiologically. Nevertheless, endoscopy is the preferred diagnostic method because an active ulcer may be difficult to identify radiologically if the duodenal bulb is scarred due to previous ulceration (Fig. 4.13). At endoscopy an ulcer will usually be visible, despite scarring and deformity of the bulb (Fig. 4.14).

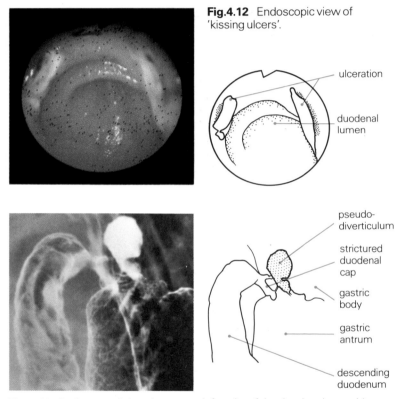

Fig. 4.12 Endoscopic view of 'kissing ulcers'.

ulceration

duodenal lumen

pseudo-diverticulum

strictured duodenal cap

gastric body

gastric antrum

descending duodenum

Fig. 4.13 Barium meal showing gross deformity of the duodenal cap with stricturing and pseudodiverticular formation making it difficult to detect a central ulcer crater.

Ulcers at, or just distal to, the junction of the first and second parts of the duodenum are known as post-bulbar ulcers. Because of their location such ulcers can be difficult to diagnose endoscopically and radiologically (Fig. 4.15).

Ulceration in the second part of the duodenum particularly when multiple or superficial, is not usually due to classical duodenal ulcer disease and suggests the possibility of Crohn's disease of the duodenum, or the Zollinger-Ellison syndrome.

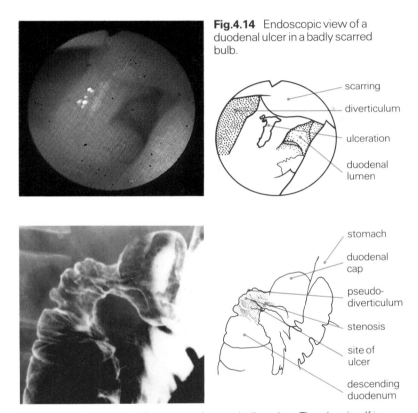

Fig.4.14 Endoscopic view of a duodenal ulcer in a badly scarred bulb.

scarring
diverticulum
ulceration
duodenal lumen

stomach
duodenal cap
pseudo-diverticulum
stenosis
site of ulcer
descending duodenum

Fig.4.15 Hypotonic duodenogram of a post-bulbar ulcer. The ulcer itself is difficult to see although the deformity with stenosis and some pseudodiverticular change is evident.

Complications of Duodenal Ulcer

The main complications of duodenal ulcer disease are haemorrhage, perforation or gastric outlet obstruction (pyloric stenosis). The risk of such complications occurring in any one individual with an ulcer is however, relatively small and has been estimated at less than one per cent per year of follow-up after the initial diagnosis.

HAEMORRHAGE

Bleeding from a duodenal ulcer occurs in 15 to 20% of patients followed up for fifteen to twenty-five years. Haemorrage is most commonly a dramatic event, with a sudden onset of haematemesis and melaena, although occasionally the bleeding is insidious, leading to an iron deficiency anaemia. The value of a barium examination in this situation is decreased because the lesion may be obscured by blood clot and

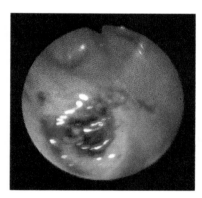 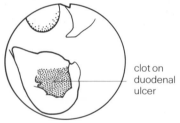

Fig.4.16 Endoscopic view of a duodenal ulcer with a clot adherent to the base. Courtesy of Dr. F. Silverstein.

clot on duodenal ulcer

patients are frequently unable to cooperate adequately with the radiologist. Endoscopy is therefore the preferred method of diagnosis, but even here blood in the gastric lumen in the actively bleeding patient may obscure the view and make the identification of the source of bleeding difficult, or impossible. Whichever method is used early diagnosis does not however, seem to affect the outcome, which is dependent on skilled management.

At endoscopy a number of stigmata of recent haemorrhage may be visible, such as actively spurting vessels, blood clot covering the ulcer (Fig. 4.16), a protruding vessel (Fig. 4.17) or a red spot in the ulcer base (Fig. 4.18). The presence of a visible vessel in the ulcer base is an important prognostic factor, because such ulcers carry a high risk of rebleeding.

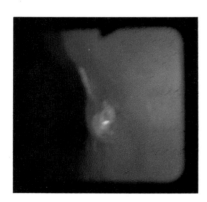

Fig.4.17 Endoscopic view of an ulcer with a protruding vessel.

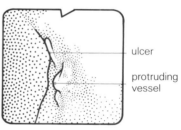

ulcer

protruding vessel

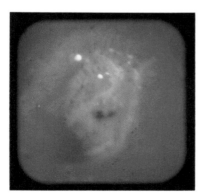

Fig.4.18 Endoscopic view of an ulcer with a red spot in its base.

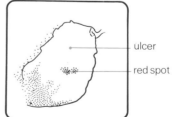

ulcer

red spot

Extension of the ulcerating process beyond the duodenal wall results in either a free perforation into the peritoneal cavity, or in penetration into an adjacent viscus. Free perforation occurs most commonly through the anterior wall of the duodenum. This is a dramtic event with a sudden onset of severe abdominal pain, followed by signs of peritonitis. A high proportion of patients have no history dyspepsia prior to the perforation. A plain abdominal radiograph taken with the patient standing and showing a crescent of intra-abdominal air beneath the diaphragm is useful confirmation of the diagnosis (Fig. 4.19).

Penetration of an ulcer most often occurs into the pancreas, but omentum, bile duct, or liver may also be involved. In this situation the history of duodenal ulcer pain is often longstanding and with the onset of penetration the pain becomes more severe and intractable. Other manifestations, such as pancreatitis, or jaundice may also arise, depending upon the site and extent of the penetration.

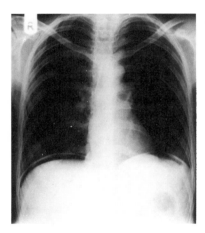

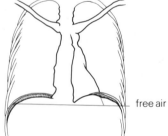

Fig.4.19 Radiograph showing free air under both diaphragms following a perforated duodenal ulcer.

free air

GASTRIC OUTLET OBSTRUCTION (PYLORIC STENOSIS)

Gastric outlet obstruction is a less common complication than either haemorrhage, or perforation. Most patients have a long history of ulcer disease, which over the years has resulted in scarring and narrowing of the pyloric canal, or of the duodenal cap. More acute ulcers with marked inflammation and oedema may give rise to similar, if less severe symptoms. The main symptom of pyloric outlet obstruction is vomiting. The vomitus characteristically contains stale food, is repetitive, and occcasionally projectile. In severe cases patients can develop metabolic alkalosis. The physical signs of pyloric stenosis include an audible succussion splash more than four hours after eating and visible gastric peristalsis.

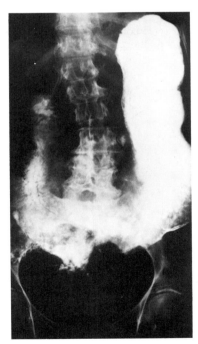

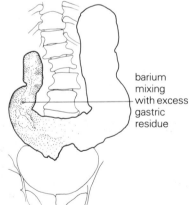

Fig.4.20 Barium meal in gastric outlet obstruction with gross dilatation of the stomach and excess gastric residue.

barium mixing with excess gastric residue

Endoscopy should only be done with caution and after the stomach has been washed out in order to lessen the risk of pulmonary aspiration of gastric contents. A pin-hole pylorus which fails to admit even 'paediatric' endoscopes may be visible. In such situations a barium meal may be more helpful and show an atonic, often dilated stomach, containing food residue (Fig. 4.20). Other causes of outlet obstruction such as adult pyloric muscle hypertrophy (Fig. 4.21), or antral neoplasm may also be defined on barium or endoscopic examination (Fig. 4.22).

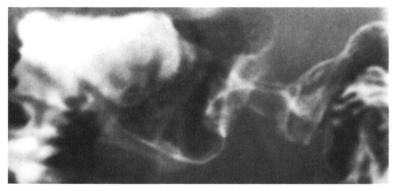

Fig.4.21 Barium meal showing pyloric stenosis due to hypertrophy of the pyloric muscle.

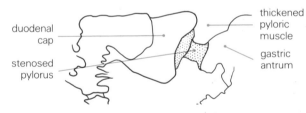

duodenal cap
stenosed pylorus
thickened pyloric muscle
gastric antrum

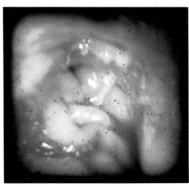

Fig.4.22 Endoscopic view of an antral neoplasm causing pyloric obstruction.

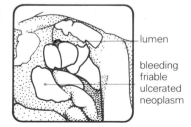

lumen

bleeding friable ulcerated neoplasm

140

Duodenitis

It is not certain whether duodenitis (duodenal inflammation) is always associated with duodenal ulceration, or whether it is a distinct entity. Patients with duodenitis may have symptoms similar to those of a duodenal ulcer, or be asymptomatic. Duodenitis can be recognised endoscopically as areas of hyperaemia and congestion (Fig.4.23) progressing in more severe cases to irregularity of the mucosa and superficial erosions (Fig.4.24). These appearances can be seen during

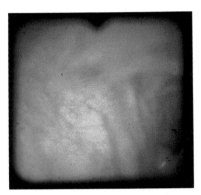

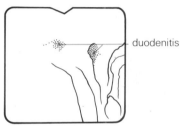

Fig.4.23 Endoscopic view of mild duodenitis showing hyperaemic areas against the background of paler duodenal mucosa.

duodenitis

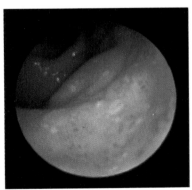

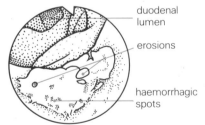

Fig.4.24 Endoscopic view of severe duodenitis showing an area of inflammation with haemorrhagic spots and erosions.

duodenal lumen

erosions

haemorrhagic spots

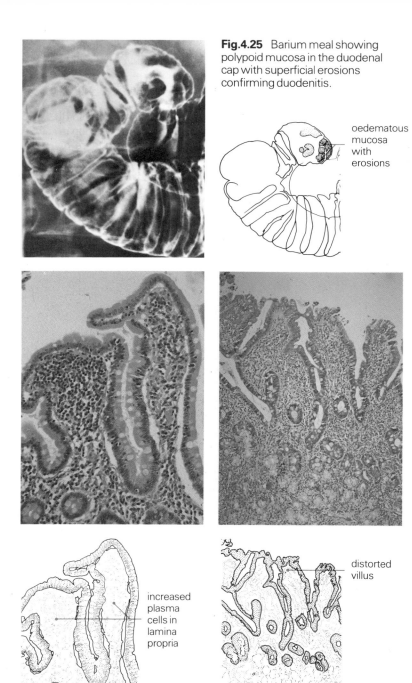

Fig.4.25 Barium meal showing polypoid mucosa in the duodenal cap with superficial erosions confirming duodenitis.

oedematous mucosa with erosions

increased plasma cells in lamina propria

distorted villus

142

the healing phase of duodenal ulcer disease. Coarse, irregular mucosal folds and erosions may be visible radiologically in the more severe forms of duodenitis (Fig. 4.25).

Although there is no endoscopic, or radiological system of grading duodenitis, histologically the appearances are classified on a scale from 0 to 3. This is based on the inflammatory cell infiltrate within the lamina propria and the degree of villous abnormality. Good clinicopathological correlations can be made in grade 3, when neutrophils are prominent along with definite villous changes (Fig. 4.26).

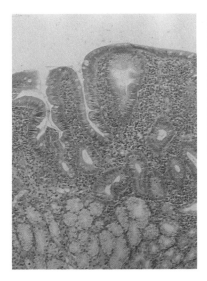

Fig.4.26 Histological appearances in duodenitis. In grade I duodenities (left, x 125) there are increased numbers of plasma cells in the lamina propria. In grade II (middle, x 50) the inflammation is beginning to distort the villous architecture. In grade III (right, x 70) the villous pattern is lost and the lamina propria is heavily infiltrated by inflammatory cells. H & E stain.

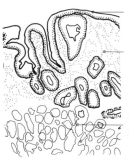

flattened villi

dense inflammatory infilrate

Brunner's glands

Duodenal Diverticula

Duodenal diverticula are pouches that protrude from the duodenal lumen. They may be congenital or acquired. Acquired diverticula are related to scarring and adhesions from peptic ulcer disease (Fig. 4.27). The majority of diverticula are congenital and arise from the second part of the duodenum within one to two centimetres of the papilla of Vater. These diverticula are frequently single, but multiple diverticula do occur (Fig. 4.28).

Stasis within large multiple diverticula in the small intestine can lead to bacterial overgrowth. This may result in malabsorption due to

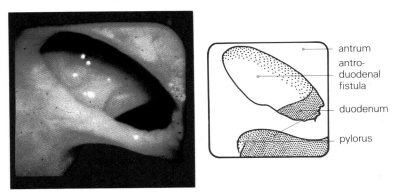

Fig. 4.27 Endoscopic view of a gastro-duodenal fistula and diverticulum caused by a previous antral ulcer in an elderly woman. The appearance is that of a 'double pylorus'. Courtesy of Dr. D. P. Jewell.

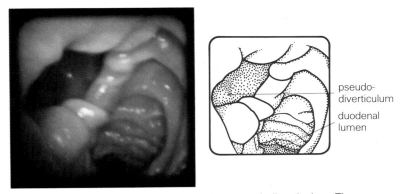

Fig. 4.28 Endoscopic view of a juxtapapillary pseudodiverticulum. The papilla is sited just inside the diverticulum.

deconjugation of bile salts, or a macrocytic anaemia due to bacterial consumption of vitamin B_{12} and interference with the vitamin B_{12}/intrinsic factor complex.

A juxtapapillary diverticulum with the papilla positioned within, or on the edge of the diverticulum may occasionally obstruct the lower end of the common bile duct, or lead to recurrent pancreatitis (Fig. 4.29). However, such diverticula are more commonly associated with the presence of stones within the common bile duct. It is not known whether they contribute to the formation of such stones, or are a result of their presence within the biliary system.

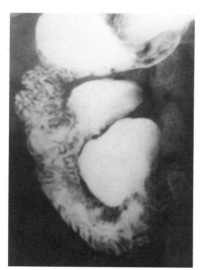

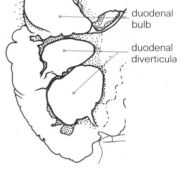

Fig.4.29 Barium meal showing two large duodenal diverticula arising from the medial border of the descending duodenum.

duodenal bulb

duodenal diverticula

Duodenal Polyps

A variety of polyps and polypoid tumours can arise in the duodenum, although they are all uncommon. Two familial conditions which give rise to intestinal polyps are Peutz-Jegher's and Gardner's syndromes.

Brunner's gland hyperplasia can occur in the first and second parts of the duodenum. This may occasionally produce a polypoid lesion which is usually only an incidental finding on a barium meal, or at endoscopy.

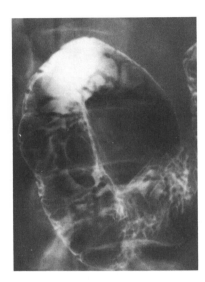

Fig.4.30 A villous adenoma surrounding the ampulla shown by hypotonic duodenography in a patient with familial polyposis coli.

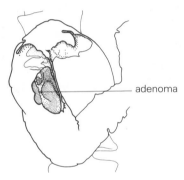

adenoma

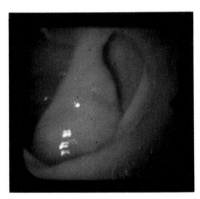

Fig.4.31 Endoscopic view of a duodenal polyp.

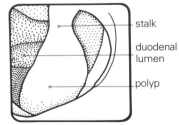

stalk

duodenal lumen

polyp

Other lesions which may present a polypoid appearance are lipomas, leiomyomas and adenomas. Complications of such polyps include bleeding and obstruction of the duodenum or (rarely), of the bile duct.

Duodenal polyps are best visualised by a barium meal (Fig.4.30) or endoscopy (Fig.4.31) and if necessary they can be snared and removed through the endoscope (Fig.4.32).

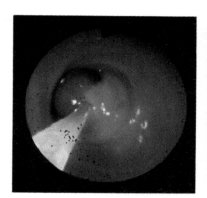 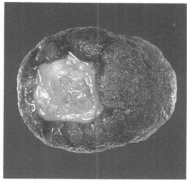

Fig.4.32 Endoscopic view of a polyp being snared (left) and the polyp following removal (right). The surface of the polyp ulcerated causing acute gastrointestinal bleeding.

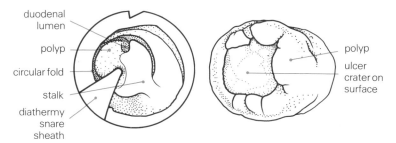

Figure 4.33 shows a resection specimen with a polyp arising from the second part.

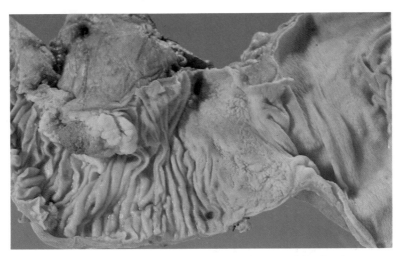

Fig.4.33 Macroscopic appearance of a villous adenoma of the duodenum.

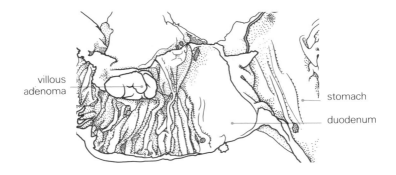

The histological appearance was that of a villous adenoma (Fig. 4.34).

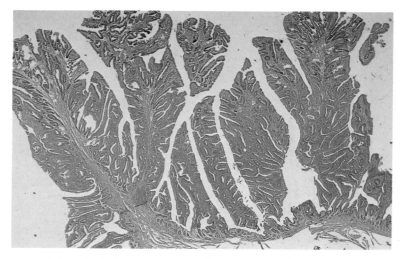

Fig.4.34 Histological appearance of a villous adenoma of the duodenum showing fronds of dysplastic mucosa but no invasion. H & E stain, x 30.

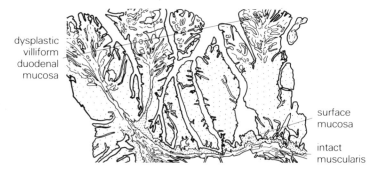

dysplastic
villiform
duodenal
mucosa

surface
mucosa

intact
muscularis

Index

lower oesophageal   5, 59, 84
oesophageal   40
pressure   55
upper oesophageal   40
Stomach   11ff
Stones, biliary system   145
Stricture   30ff, 44
formation 59
oesophageal   61f
'Sump' ulcer   80
Surgery, gastric   118ff
Swallowing   5ff, 54

T

Thrombosis, portal vein   66
Trichobezoar   124
Trypanosoma cruzi   54
Tumour, oesophageal   47
polypoid   146

U

Ulcer, duodenal   119, 131
complications   136ff
haemorrhage   136f
perforation   136, 138
Ulcer, gastric   72ff
benign   72ff
benign giant   78
complications   83
exclusion of malignancy   81f
greater curve   80
juxtapyloric   79
malignant   80ff
perforation   38

U

Ulcer, post-bulbar   135
Ulcer, peptic   115, 118
Ulcer, oesophageal   30, 37f, 64

V

Vagus, fibre types   16
Vagus nerve   16, 24
Varices, oesophageal   66f
Vomiting, gastric diverticula
symptom   115
pyloric stenosis symptom   139

W

Web, oesophageal   52f

Z

Z line   8
Zenker's diverticulum   40
Zollinger-Ellison syndrome   119,
133, 135